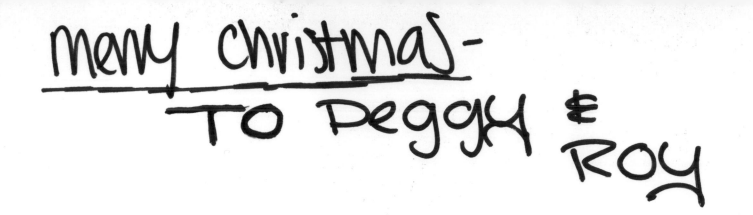

Merry Christmas-
To Peggy & Roy

Love,
Rachel
Trean

08'

OVER AMERICA

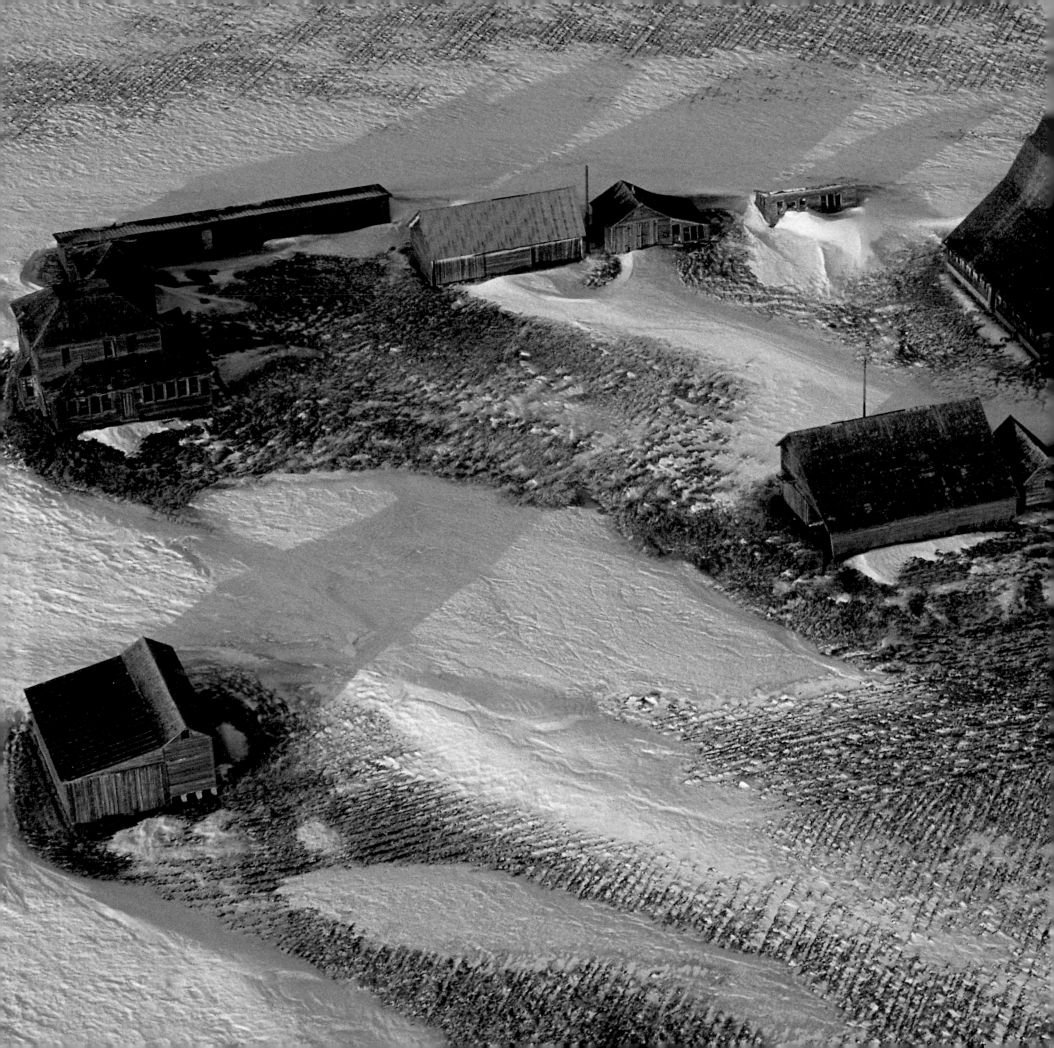

OVER AMERICA

INTRODUCTION
BY
ANDREI CODRESCU

FOG CITY PRESS

Published by Fog City Press
814 Montgomery Street
San Francisco, CA 94133 USA

Copyright © 2003 Weldon Owen Pty Ltd

Chief Executive Officer: John Owen
President: Terry Newell
Publisher: Lynn Humphries
Creative Director: Sue Burk
Editorial Coordinator: Kiren Thandi
Production Manager: Caroline Webber
Production Coordinator: James Blackman
Sales Manager: Emily Jahn
Vice President International Sales: Stuart Laurence

Project Coordinator: Jessica Cox
Project Designer: Jacqueline Richards
Regional Introductions: Luba Vangelova
Captions: Jessica Cox, Mark Derr, T. R. Fehrenbach, Steven Goldsberry, Jim Klobuchar,
Murray Morgan, Neal R. Pierce, Kevin Starr, Luba Vangelova

ISBN 978-1-877019-65-4

Color reproduction by SC (Sang Choy) International Pte Ltd
Printed by LeeFung-Asco Printers
Printed in China

A Weldon Owen Production

Captions
Page 1: Wyoming, the country's least-populated state, has vast areas of contrasting wilderness,
including erosion-sculpted "badlands," rolling high plains and alpine mountains.
Pages 2–3: A ghost farmyard near Heron Lake in Jackson County, Minnesota, gives the appearance
of an old fort under the assault of winter. The architecture and aging wood provide a glimpse
of farms as they were before modern materials changed the face of the American farmyard.
Right: A view looking over Manana Island to Makapuu Point, Oahu, Hawaii. The point is a popular
spot for watching Northern Pacific humpback whales pass through the Molokai Channel as they
migrate south from their summer home in the waters off the Aleutian islands.

CONTENTS

AMERICA: A PERSONAL ODYSSEY

I came to America on a chartered plane full of immigrants who started chanting, "America! America!" when the coastline of Nova Scotia slid into view. The morning sun had gold-leafed the scalloped shore like a Christmas present. The church steeples of New England glinted from the snow, bespeaking an orderly world, still tied by tradition to the Europe we had left behind. Nonetheless, even from this height there was already something more open, more fearless and more prosperous about this coastline, these villages and fields. The land was not surrounded by fortifications; it did not look out with suspicion over battlements. Centuries of immigrants had preceded me, but those huddled masses arriving by ship had never been presented with such a glorious nation. America was to become my new home, though I didn't know yet exactly where in it I would live.

The slight kinship of the New World with the Old evaporated soon enough. The pilot banked his big bird over New York and the view became indelible in my memory. The Statue of Liberty came into view, her image slipping quite easily into the space already reserved for her in our minds. We had seen her so many times in pictures that she had a home already there, behind our eyes. The towers of Manhattan's skyline thrust upward into the cloudless blue sky, proclaiming their resolute break with old Europe. New York was tall and erect, whereas the cities of Europe had lain lazily, hugging the ground. America proclaimed its vigor and energy with the exclamation point of her skyscrapers. The canyons between were filled with the turbulent rage of torrents of cars, and millions of windows sparkled in the sun.

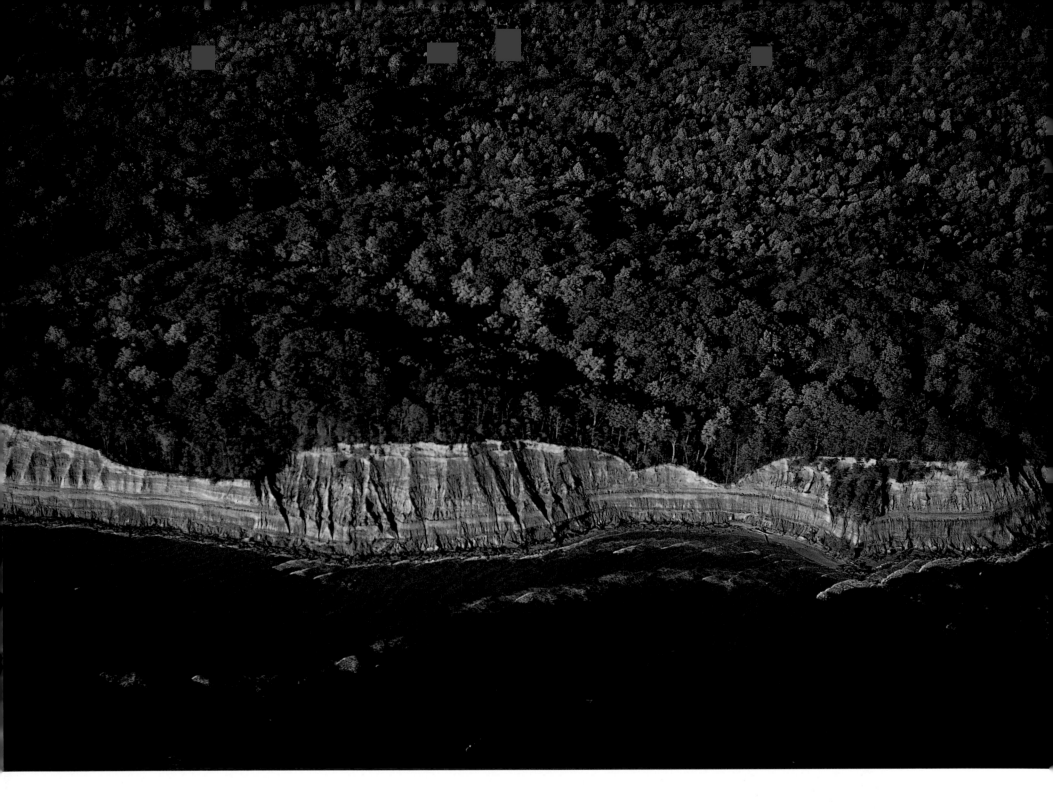

CHESAPEAKE BAY, Maryland

Autumn colors complement the distinctive sediment layers in Maryland's Calvert Cliffs. Rising more than 100 feet above the Chesapeake Bay, the cliffs harbor a treasure trove of shark teeth, whale bones, seashells and other fossils dating back millions of years, to when this area was a submerged tropical seafloor.

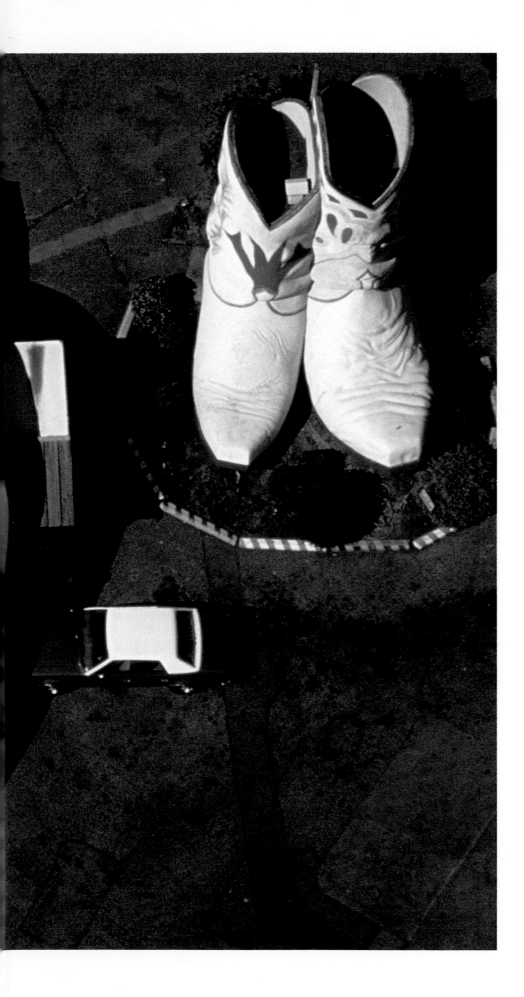

I must have flown into New York dozens of times from every direction since then, but I still get a slight chill of wonder at its unapologetic pride. Manhattan's towers are emblematic of a century of industrial might, supreme confidence and entrepreneurial spirit. The raw muscle and imagination of America's immigrants made a powerful impression here. I see a fleet of buses at rest, sleek like plump seals, ready to stream into the dynamic streets of the great city. And in another image, the electric nerves of the metropolis, glowing with the flush of material well-being. No matter what gloomy thoughts I subsequently had in New York, the city where I ended up living for two years, these pictures revive in me that first feeling of fearless liberty. New York City is seen best from the air because its citizens already live and work high above its skyscrapers, and the city tends continually upward. "Going up" and "moving up" are true American metaphors, enclosing the ever-upward urge that finds its purest embodiment in the city of Walt Whitman, the poet who proudly called himself "the son of Manhattan."

SEATTLE, Washington

Seen here in its heyday, the Hat and Boot gas station is a Seattle landmark. With the hat as the gas station and the boots as restrooms, the structure gained national attention when it was built in the 1950s. Today, with locals and government officials at an impasse over its future, the Hat and Boot sits unused and falling into decay.

CAPE CANAVERAL, Florida (above)

The John F. Kennedy Space Center is located near Florida's Cape Canaveral spaceport, from which space shuttles and moon missions have been launched since it was established in 1962. The grounds contain evidence of the site's history, such as the "missile garden," shown above.

LAKE POWELL, Arizona (right)

Lake Powell, stretching from northern Arizona into southern Utah, was formed by the Glen Canyon Dam, built in the 1960s to control the flow of the Colorado River and to generate hydroelectricity. Tourists explore the lake and its surrounding canyonlands on houseboats.

"The central fact of man in North America is SPACE," wrote the poet Charles Olson, speaking of the insight of earlier American and fellow New Englander, Herman Melville. In truth, Space, in its large and generous amplitude, does not begin until one heads north and west. After a stop at Kennedy Airport, the refugee plane took off for Detroit, where the Jewish Refugee Organization (HIAS) was prepared to welcome yet another passel of hopeful souls to America's generous vastness. We passed over rivers banked by both working and idle giant industrial factories, and looked down on large farms covered with comforters of deep snow under which the world's bounty of grain slept in expectation of spring.

Detroit itself came into view carrying the grime of industrial age like a heavy mantle. The Rouge River was frozen, but the smokestacks of the River Rouge plant wrote in the sky a message that must have lifted the spirits of hundreds of thousands of Eastern European immigrants for more than a century: "There is work! The engines are humming!"

Or so it seemed to me, in those almost-innocent days of the mid-1960s before the oil embargo, inflation and the popularity of Japanese cars.

The views of the Midwest in this book speak both the story of those innocent days and the subsequent history. The Great Lakes, these inland seas, float mighty ships filled with the riches of the land that surround them. The patterns of wheat, corn, sunflower, mustard, soy and alfalfa are firmly drawn. One can easily see from the air the plenitude that has caught the attention of the world's hungry. In the novel *The Pit* by Frank Norris, a madman decided to corner the Midwestern wheat market, gambling on a meagre harvest. The repercussions are widespread: there is famine in Europe and distress elsewhere. But the earth, resplendent in her independence and resentful in her selfishness, brings forth an abundant crop. The designs of the arrogant trader are undermined, buried under waves and waves of wheat. From the air, one can see all the relationships at once: that of farmer to the land, of land to the harvest, of harvest to boundary. One realizes, above all, that humility is the proper response to the land. And after that, joy and thanksgiving.

NEWPORT, Rhode Island

The Breakers, a mansion built of a dozen types of alabaster and marble, dominates the neighboring "cottages" at Ochre Point. Conceived by wealthy southerners before the Civil War, the "cottages" of Newport were built by plantation owners, railroad magnates and self-made, ostentatious Northern capitalists in the nineteenth century.

The bold skyline of Chicago sprawls like the signature of a bank guarantor for all this wealth. The buildings of Chicago display no false modesty as the efficacy of commercial purpose mingles with the daring of modern architecture. The hypocritical scruples of the Old World, which deemed its opera houses more refined than its banks, are gone here. From the air, Chicago displays its contrasts in character, from its shiny railways like a workman's veins to the ostentatiously fancy dress of its transparent towers. Chicago also aims to live in its skyscrapers and move up but, unlike New York, it is more firmly connected to the commodities that fuel its growth. The penthouses of Chicago's towers still smell of loam and crushed grain; they share a spirit with the silos that surround them in the darkness of the countryside.

America's industry is more visible in the Midwest, but the shapes and aims of the land have not been completely buried by the efforts of modern Americans. In Ohio, the Great Serpent Mound is witness to an Amerindian civilization of which little is known beyond the massive monuments that stretch as far south as Mississippi. Even the history of the westward migration is still visible, in the form of scars on the land left by covered wagons on the Oregon Trail.

Traveling by car, the intimacy of each bend in the road is reassuring. You can stop and take the measure of a place, revel in its particulars. Each letter or syllable of the topography stands alone, its relation to others not very clear. From the air, however, the patterns of nature and the works of humanity mingle to make sentences, phrases, chapters. Together, the infinite variations of this country combine to form a story.

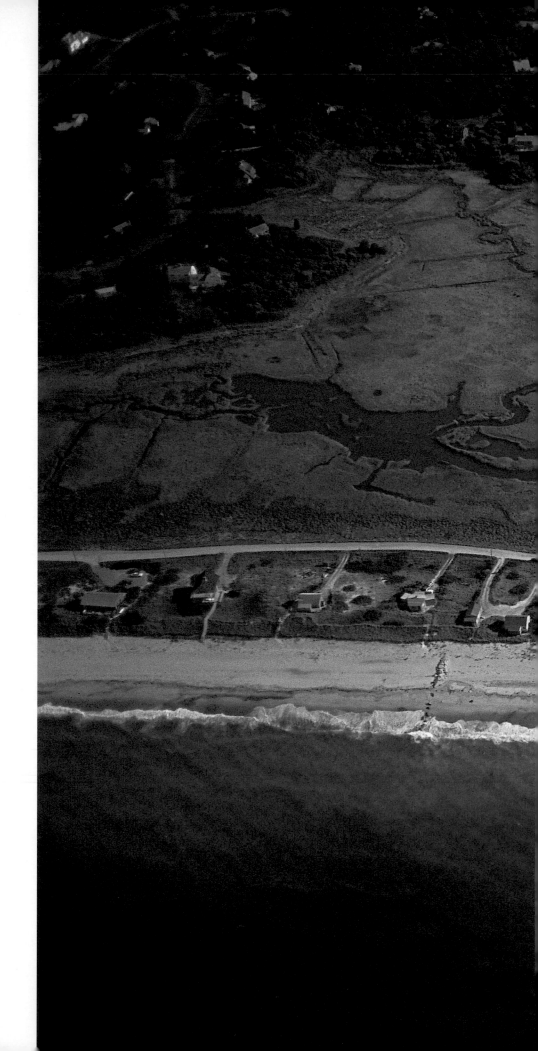

Cities, of course, tell their stories in lights. The quiet towns
tell an orderly story, lights shining out of their windows
with the disciplined glow of work and self-control. After
the 10 or 11 o'clock news, their lights turn off at once,
leaving only traffic lights to keep watch over them. Other
cities, chief among which is Las Vegas, tell a different story
with blinding and party-colored neon. Las Vegas, like Coney
Island at night, sends up messages of guilt-free joy that
look like whirling loops, spinning rings and geysers. If this
book contained no more than nocturnal views, its photos
would still be cause for astonishment.

North America uses a staggering amount of electricity to
keep her cities illuminated at night. And yet, after all that
expense and energy, the continent is dark for most of the
part. The illuminated oases of the cities are only little dots
on the great map of the continent. North America, despite
the cries of alarm raised by those panicked by the sprawl
of human civilization, is still mostly wood, mountain,
desert, farm and water.

Deciphering the various messages of the American landscape
requires an eclectic knowledge, but it also involves fancy
and imagination: in the clouds one can read the sometimes
playful, sometimes painful script. Looking up at the clouds

CAPE COD, Massachusetts

The earliest settlers of Cape Cod made a living from fishing.
Boat builders, saltmakers, cranberry farmers and whalers followed
in their wake. The area's dune-lined beaches and well-preserved
villages are now a favorite summer destination for New Englanders,
despite the water's chilly temperatures.

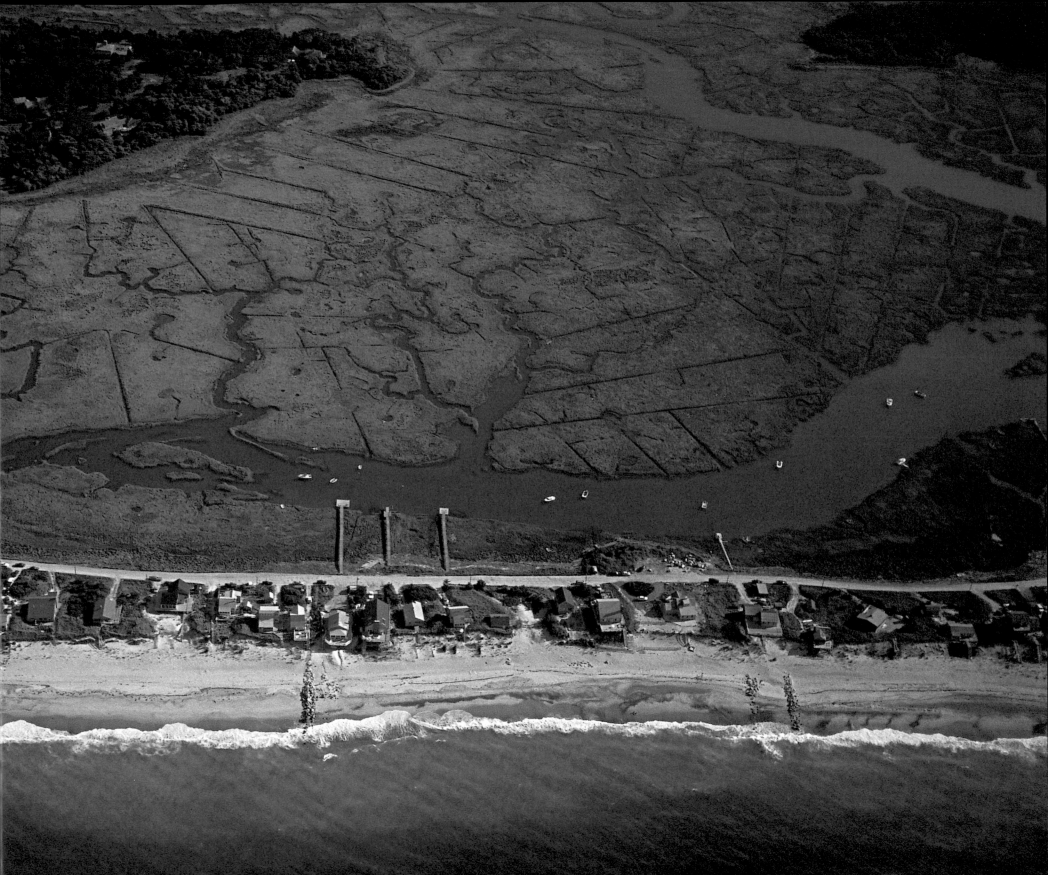

is very much like looking down from them. When my children were young, we used to lie in the grass and see everything we ever knew or could think of by looking at the clouds. The earth spinned with us and we with it and the stories of the sky were infinite. It isn't much different looking down from a plane onto the enigmatic and evocative formations of the South West, to see our most intimate images reflected there. The reach and limitations of the human imagination become quickly evident above the Grand Canyon, for instance.

Standing at Hopi Point on the South Rim of the Grand Canyon at sunset, I knew for certain that the earth was

CHACO CULTURE NATIONAL HISTORICAL PARK, New Mexico

Located at the northern edge of Chaco Canyon, Pueblo Bonito is the largest and one of the most significant sites in the Chaco complex. Archaeologists believe the structure, built in stages between 850 and 1250 AD, was a public building used for ceremonies and as temporary housing for itinerant groups when they traveled to Chaco for trade.

greater than all human works. I knew
also, beyond a shadow of doubt, that
I preferred America to the Europe
I had left behind. "The poetry of the
earth is never dead," wrote John
Keats, but in Europe the earth had
been tamed, the wilderness made
sensible. Here in America was the
romantic vision of Keats and the
dreamscape of Coleridge's "caverns
measureless to man." The complex
grandeur of what lay below was an
argument without rebuttal. The
mountains and buttes were awash in
color. Layers of mineral and fossil
rock told of a timeless geological
past. The peaks and valleys below
had their own weather. The human
story, told in rock paintings,
carvings, and artifacts, began

KONA, Hawaii

An outrigger canoe paddling team trains
in the smooth, aquamarine shallows of a
reef near Kona, on the western coast of
Hawaii's Big Island. Traditionally, large,
double-hulled canoes were used by the
Polynesians for traveling, and held whole
families, dogs, pigs, chickens, water gourds,
coconuts, sweet potatoes and kukui nuts.
Today, canoeing has become a popular
sport with tourists and locals alike.

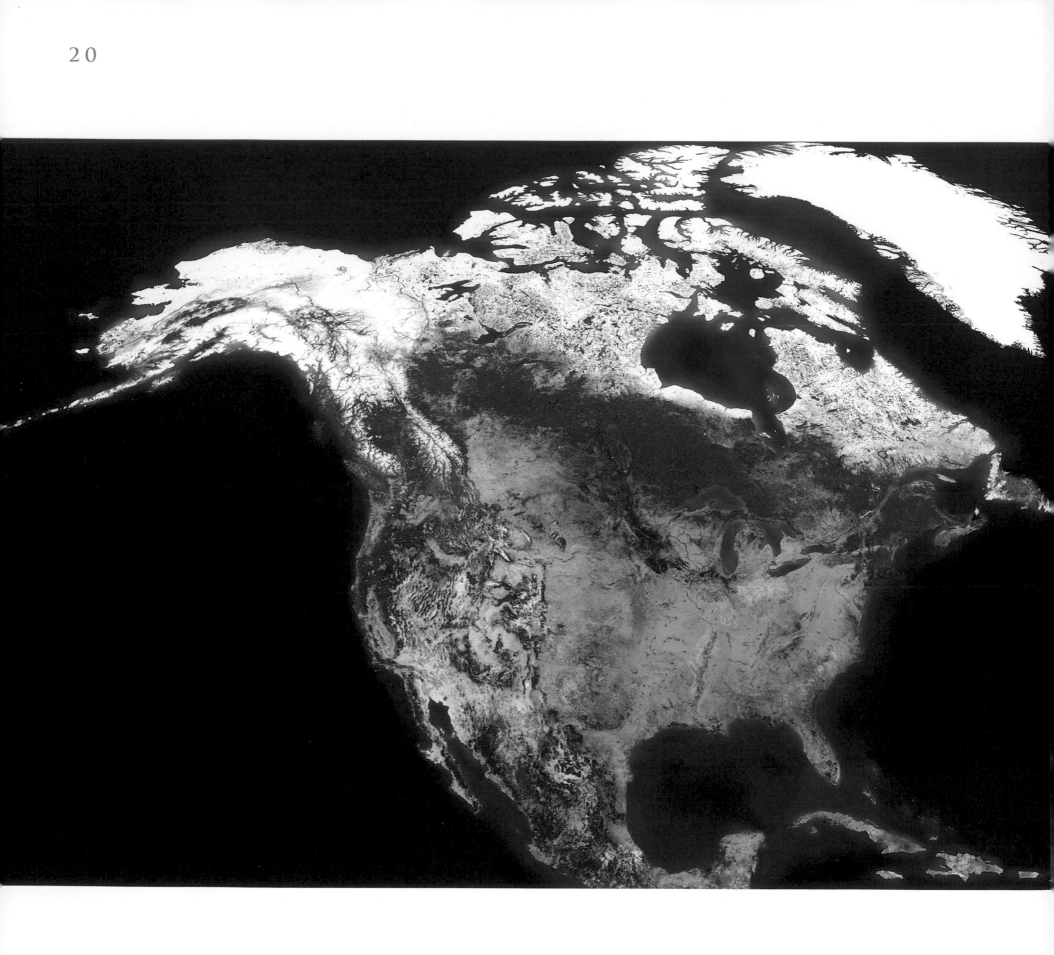

with the Archaic People of 2500 BC and moved on to the Anasazi of AD 1100 through the Havasupai and Hopis in the 1800s, to the Navajos in the 1900s. Here was space, revealed from within, a gift from Mother Earth to me. Francisco Vásquez de Coronado, the first white man to have seen the canyon in 1540, thought that he had found the seven Cities of Gold, *El Dorado.* Subsequently, men whose imaginations failed them named the mountains and formations of the Grand Canyon after the castles, temples and gods of the Old World. Below me lay Isis, Buda, Deva, Brahma and Zoroaster, mountains named after the most awesome creations of the mystic imagination. This heroic nomenclature fails to convey the grandeur of the site because the landscape is irreducible itself, a masterwork of the Colorado River and of the sky. I could see how other metaphors might proceed from it, but not the other way around. This was a Source.

Walt Whitman wrote, "Something startles me where I thought I was safest." The landscape of North America often mocks our human-measured notion of safety and scale. Early English travelers did not like America. It was too big and

unmanageable. To British writer Frances Trollope, Niagara Falls was "an accompaniment to conversation" and Oscar Wilde wrote, "The sight of the stupendous waterfall must be one of the first, if not the keenest, disappointments in American married life." All effort to civilize, miniaturize and domesticize the world comes to nothing in America. Many early explorers left their bones in the desert or in the swift waters of the Colorado. I try to imagine what it must have been like to see the Grand Canyon for the first time as Francisco Vásquez de Coronado did, or to behold the Mississippi as Hernando De Soto did. For them, it must have been a lot like being airborne. The vistas must have spoken to them on a planetary scale. What they said about these natural wonders was not easily decipherable. The Hopi Indians, who discovered the canyon first, read poetry in what lay below: "The song resounds back from our Creator with joy, and we of the earth repeat it to our Creator."

After emigrating to Detroit in 1966, I did not stay put long. The siren call of the North American continent combined with the adventurous spirit of the age to drive me west. I followed the classic route of the western migrant, only I traveled by bus and car, not by air. I learned about my new country traveling mile-by-mile on endless ribbons of road, city by city. From New York to San Francisco, through prairie, mountains and deserts, I learned to appreciate her awesome dimensions. The spirits of the land grew stronger the farther west I traveled. I shared my new home with spirits that inhabited the rocks and the floors of long-vanished seas. Driving America by car I tasted the density of her roots. Had I walked I would have distinguished the even finer particulars of that density, but I would not have been able

SATELLITE VIEW, Continental North America

Weather varies greatly across continental North America. At the top of this topographical satellite image, northern Canada, Alaska and Greenland lie under a blanket of white snow and ice. The bare brown earth of deserts and mountain ranges can be seen to dominate the west coast, while the grasses of the mid-western prairies appear pale green.

to travel very far. America was meant to be seen by air. The Native Americans esteemed the eagle above all other animals because of its ability to soar and encompass.

Perspective is at the source of all knowledge. What we see depends on where we stand. Not very long ago, human beings could not see very far. I remember staring in wonder at fifteenth-century aerial views of Sibiu, my medieval hometown in Romania. These intricate drawings had been composed from the top of the highest hill overlooking the city. Proceeding from the church in the central square, the town fanned out concentrically to the fortified wall that surrounded it. Beyond the wall there was nothing to be seen. I loved finding my house (built in 1456) in those drawings.

Later, I flew in a glider over the town and found my house again, only this time it was part of an even larger shape as I was able to see the foothills that hugged the city—which had expanded far beyond its medieval walls—and the snowcapped mountains beyond that hugged the foothills. I now saw more than my grandfather, who had seen his town only from his horse, or my father, who'd driven through it in a car. For them, the shapes of the unknown landscape ahead held dangers proportional to the distances they could travel. Everything beyond the capacity of their transport was fraught with peril; it belonged to the hostile outside, the place that was not home.

In the spaces of North America, the sense of peril does not come from rival cities over the hill but from the loneliness of one's habitation. With the exception of the starbursts of cities, the North American night is dark and its dimensions are still inviolate. Finding one's home from the air in such immensity has both pathos and poetry.

I was jotting these notes on an airliner, during the approach to Philadelphia airport, when I heard a breathless young girl behind me tell her mother: "Look mom, there is our house!" The pilot was banking the plane over the snowy jigsaw puzzle below. It was February and a snowstorm had just left the area. I saw the ice on the Susquehanna River, the reactor of a nuclear plant with the white puff of steam over it like a fat dragon, an accordionlike subdivision, a white football field. Somewhere in there was that little girl's house. "There, mom!" she said, frustration building in her voice because the mother, not as quick as her daughter, hadn't spotted it yet. Perhaps the child was already endowed with a greater capacity for seeing more and in greater detail than her mother. She was at home in the air, more so than her elders who came of age when flights were still a rarity.

I live now in New Orleans, near the mouth of the Mississippi River. When you fly over the Mississippi floodplain between the river and Lake Pontchartrain into the port of New Orleans, the little patches of land that float on the water look like afterthoughts in the creation landscape. It doesn't seem like people could live on these tiny, tufted islands. But, in fact, these islands are an original thought, not an afterthought, of the big river as it moves the soil of the plains into the Gulf of Mexico. Consequently, everything that lives here, including myself, is the aftermath of the river's original thought. In this eco-region of the *Messachebe* (the Choctaw Indian name for the Mississippi), water is our

medium. We live in it, we talk of it, we are thought by it, we see the world through it.

The Mississippi, since its very first recorded sighting by De Soto in 1541, has been giving us a flood of stories exceeded only by the volume of its waters. One might say, paraphrasing Herodotus, that American literature is a gift of the Mississippi. But this magnificent river, which runs through the imaginations of children all over the world, is not one of us. In fact, it is mad at us. The flood of 1993, the largest in the river's recorded history, also flooded our national consciousness. Discussion about the river has risen steadily past the estimates of flood damage to unsettling questions about the nature

MONTEREY COUNTY, California

A dirt road leads through a canyon in the coastal hills near King City in the Salinas Valley. Brown in the summer, these hills will take on an emerald-velvet lushness after the rains come in winter. Known to many as "Steinbeck country," the Salinas Valley's fertile soils make it an important agricultural, as well as cultural, region.

of our relationship with this "strong brown god," as T.S. Eliot called it. Mark Twain, who learned the book of the river by heart, said so right from the start: "10 thousand river commissions, with the mines of the world at their back, cannot tame that lawless stream, cannot curb it or confine it, cannot say to it, 'Go here,' or 'Go there,' and make it obey; cannot save a shore which it has sentenced; cannot bar its path with an obstruction which it will not tear down, dance over and laugh at." No one listened. Since 1927, the army corps of engineers have built, dredged and dug $25 billion worth of levees, dams and channels along the Mississippi and its tributaries. We spend $2 billion each year on flood damage. There are 20 locks and dams on the river above Hannibal, Missouri, Twain's boyhood town.

Between the hilltop or mountain peak of the cartographer and the orbit of the astronaut, there are countless heights from which to see the world. They all yield a different knowledge, but they all have in common the exclamation of the

LOUDOUN COUNTY, Virginia (left)

The suburbs that line the Dulles Access Road in northern Virginia have spawned many high-technology companies. Entrepreneurs are attracted by the region's highly skilled workforce and by its proximity to one of the country's biggest-spending customers, the federal government.

TERRACE FARMS, Iowa (above)

Terraced hills combine with lush green fields and dusky trees to create abstract, yet organic, forms in the farmland of southwest Iowa. Its fertile soil has helped make Iowa the heartland of American agriculture. Today it leads the country in corn and soybean production.

little girl on the airplane: "Look, mom, there is our house!" Paradoxically, the higher we get and the more we see, the more important our specific speck of dirt becomes. It is the search for our specificity in the larger scheme of things that inspires flight. What is revealed is the pattern wherein we dwell, the coherence of the physical body.

To see from the air is to see philosophically because you see the patterns. But what is the correct height from which to see America? How high do you have to be to see the nation? What is the correct height from which to see not just geographically but politically, socially, morally?

Some years ago, the visual artist Christo, together with an Air Force general, a sheep farmer and a marine biologist, flew over parts of northern California to survey the site for Christo's sculpture Running Fence. This was the first time that these people, each one with a special interest in one aspect of the land, had seen it through each others' eyes: the home of plants, animals, marine life forms, grazing ground or a canvas for art. The sheep farmer, who had seen it only as a grazing ground, was astonished to see all its

WINONA, Minnesota

During the steamboat era, Winona was the first port of call in Minnesota for thousands of settlers and immigrants coming up the Mississippi. From its sawmill past it emerged as an important wheat shipping and trade center, and eventually a college town and destination for many Polish and German immigrants.

other faces. The marine biologist, who had seen only the life forms in the water hugging the coast, saw a different kind of diversity. But it was Christo, the artist, who brought them all together by means of a daring imaginary construct. When the white nylon fence was finally constructed, it sliced through the hills like a white wing or a sail, lifting the landscape as if it were airborne. During the time Running Fence fluttered there in the wind, everyone in the area participated in a passionate debate about the nature of the land that they had—up until that time—inhabited blindly. Seeing one's home from the air has the same effect. It brings home the realization that one's place on earth is multifaceted, complex and beautiful.

Looking on these spectacular photographs I am seized by the desire to fly in a small plane at the altitudes that make such composition possible. My aerial views have been almost exclusively from the windows of commercial airliners. At 30,000 feet, to the naked eye, the landscape yields only its major structures. Snowy alpine ridges and inland seas seem quite friendly. There is no hint of their difficulty, desolation or severity. But each height reveals a specific mystery. To the maker of weather maps, using images beamed down by satellites, patterns have precise meanings. To the nonspecialist such as myself, the wealth of forms speaks of abstraction and symmetry. I see shapes that look like alien landing pads, and the ridges, mountaintops and rivers are to me the bones, tissue and veins of the earth. It is perhaps a testimony to the ability of humans to transcend themselves that the body becomes the measure of everything we see. Still, it is true: when from on high I look at the earth below, I see a body that is partly mine.

THE NORTH EAST

CONNECTICUT ~ DELAWARE ~ MAINE ~ MASSACHUSETTS
NEW HAMPSHIRE ~ NEW JERSEY ~ NEW YORK
PENNSYLVANIA ~ RHODE ISLAND ~ VERMONT

Although the country's first European colonists settled in the South, the North East can more legitimately claim to be the cradle of the nation. This was where colonial resentments exploded into full-scale revolution, and where the ideological foundations of the United States were subsequently laid out.

This geographically diverse region encompasses the New England states—Maine, Vermont, New Hampshire, Connecticut, Rhode Island and Massachusetts—and the northern Mid-Atlantic states of New York, New Jersey, Pennsylvania and Delaware.

The region's first settlers were English Pilgrims who sailed to Plymouth, Massachusetts, in 1620 to escape religious persecution. They were prepared to govern themselves, but less prepared to survive New England's harsh winters. Yet they persevered, with the help of friendly Native Americans. But relations between natives and colonists did not remain permanently troublefree, and subsequent waves of European settlers gradually dispossessed the indigenous tribes until the latter all but disappeared from the region.

Relatively few Yankees, as New Englanders call themselves, can trace their lineage to the Pilgrims. But many more pride themselves on a similar tenacity and steadfast work ethic. A quest for self-improvement—financial if not spiritual—underpinned achievements such as the founding of many world-class institutions of higher learning.

LAKES REGION, New Hampshire

New Hampshire's mountainous countryside, dotted with hundreds of lakes and ponds, has made the state popular with hikers, skiers, boaters and other tourists. Well might Robert Frost, whose homestead in Derry, New Hampshire, is now a national historic landmark, write: "It is restful just to think about New Hampshire."

BRADFORD, Vermont (above)

Vermont's pastoral beauty draws many visitors to the state, whose economy is heavily dependent on tourism as well as agriculture. Field crops such as these near Bradford, on the banks of the Connecticut River, are vital to Vermont's dairy industry. Much of Vermont's "white gold" supplies the urban populations of Boston and New York.

ARCADIA NATIONAL PARK, Maine (right)

The pink granite slopes of Arcadia National Park in northern Maine drape the Atlantic horizon. The Abenaki Indians knew this place as *Pemetic*, "the sloping land." When Samuel de Champlain sailed by in 1604 he called it *L'Isle des monts*, "island of bare mountains." Hundreds of bird species, rare plants and solitary humans find the landscape to their liking.

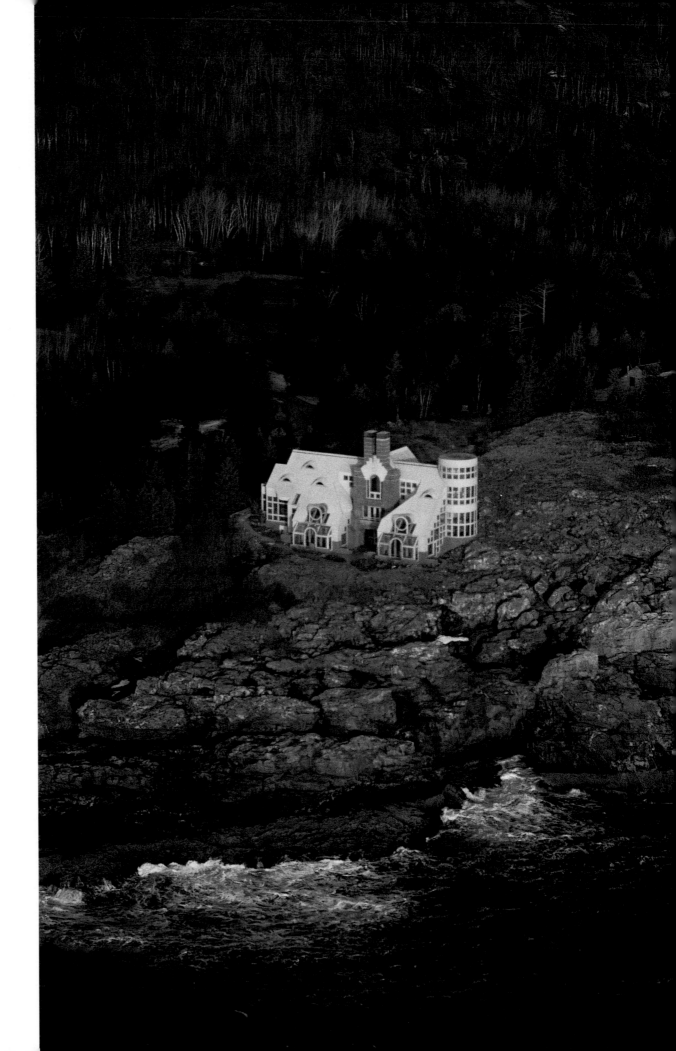

A respect for independent thought and action also made Boston, Massachusetts, a hotbed of colonial resistance to English authority. Political action eventually gave way to armed revolt, and the first shots of the War of Independence were to be fired in nearby Lexington, Massachusetts, in April 1775. Other key events in the new nation's early history—such as the drafting of the U.S. Constitution in Philadelphia, Pennsylvania—were recorded in this region. It is a heritage that today's residents still cherish, as evidenced by the popularity of the area's well-tended historic sites.

The region's cities attract immigrants from around the world. Boston marks the northern tip of a string of large urban areas that have nearly coalesced into one giant megalopolis, stretching some 500 miles. Prime among these is New York, which, with a population of 8 million, is the nation's largest city. Seen as a gateway into America, New York is a giant mixing bowl of ideas, fashions, cultures and beliefs. Its influence, like that of the nation that sprang up in this region, now spans the globe.

CEMETERY, Rhode Island

Rhode Island was established in 1635
by Roger Williams, an outcast from the
Massachusetts Bay Colony to the north
because of his views on religious freedom.
The state prospered from shipping and
international trade and became one of
the country's most fashionable millionaires'
playgrounds in the late nineteenth century.
This windswept cemetery, bleak in the
depths of winter, may be the final resting
place for some of the state's founders.

FARMLAND, New York (left)

New York State is often equated with the large metropolitan area that shares its name. But much of the state, outside of its mountainous regions, is rich agricultural land, whose farmers benefit from their proximity to such a large urban market. Here, an old-fashioned hedgerow separates fall field from the harvest.

PITTSBURGH, Pennsylvania (right)

Pittsburgh reigned supreme as the center of America's industrial might for a century, until the steel industry virtually collapsed in the 1970s. Since then, the once-polluted city has become better known for its cultural, educational and medical institutions, and consistently rates as one of America's most livable cities.

POPHAM BEACH STATE PARK,
Maine

Popham Beach, located at the mouth of
the Kennebec River in southern Maine, is
so named because of George Popham who
attempted to build the first European
settlement in North America here in 1607.
Following a severe winter, and the death of
Popham, the settlers returned to England
disheartened. The salt-tolerant marshes,
pictured, reflect the harshness of the New
England climate. The olive-colored moss
is prized by florists.

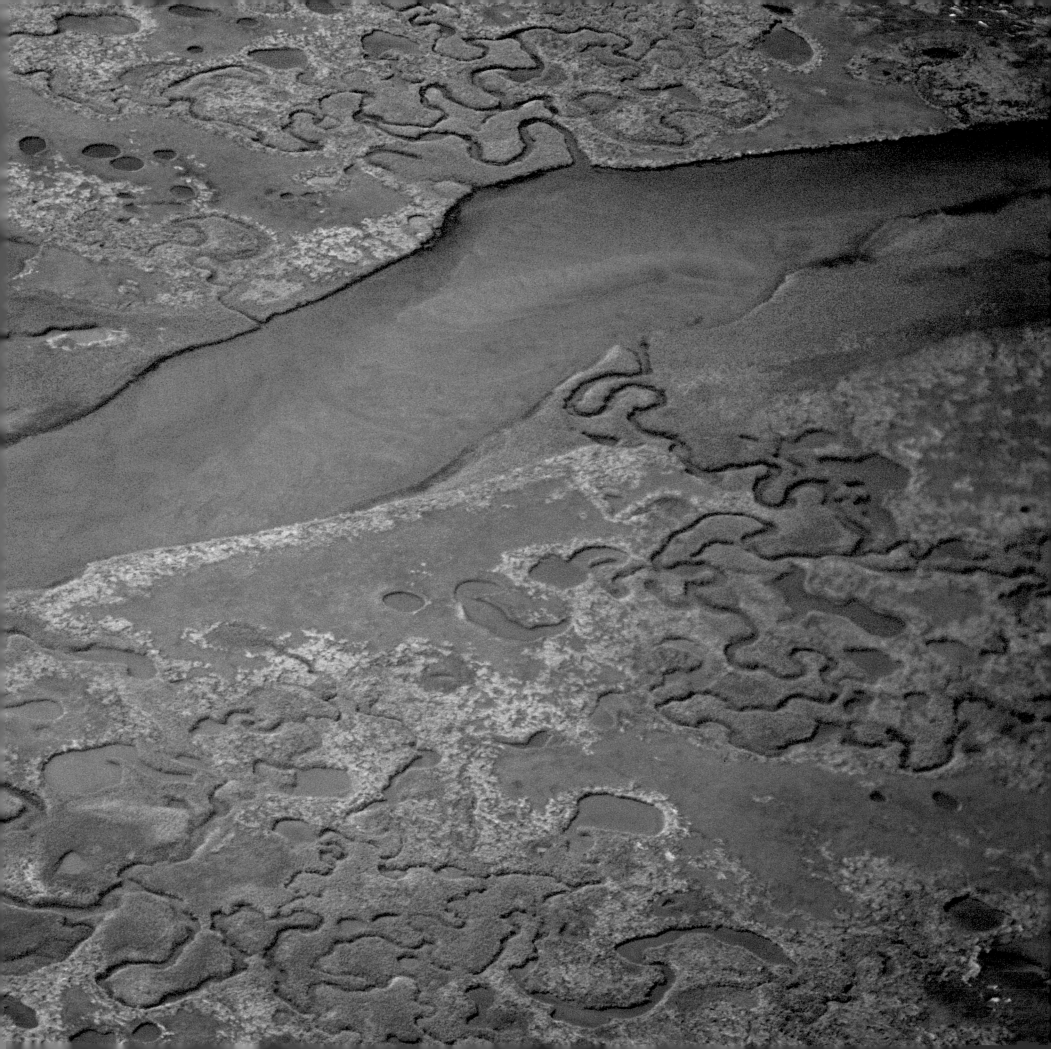

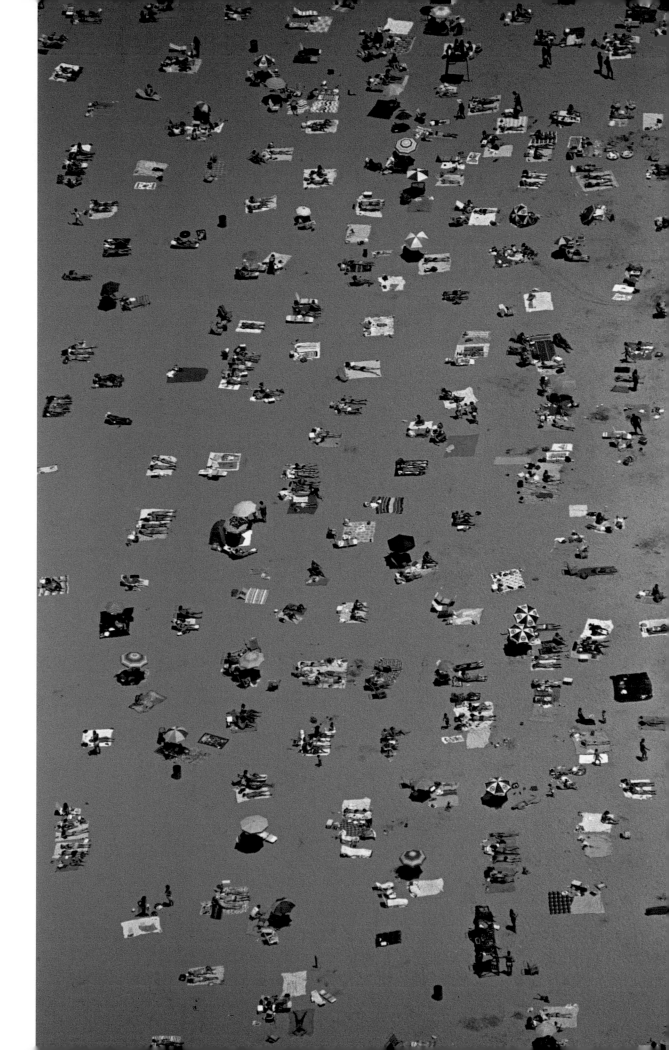

WINDSOR COUNTY, Vermont (left)

This mysterious stone chamber south of Woodstock is believed by some to predate European settlement of the area. The chamber's entrance is constructed to align with the sun during the winter solstice, when its interior is spectacularly filled with sunlight. Standing stones with other possible astronomical significance dot the surrounding countryside.

LONG ISLAND SOUND, Connecticut (right)

Pleasure Beach at Bridgewater on Long Island Sound is aptly named, its sands and sea providing a respite for nearby residents and visitors alike. While the water quality of Long Island is an ongoing community issue, local and federal environmental protection agencies are working together to restore the ecosystem.

BOMBAY HOOK NATIONAL WILDLIFE REFUGE, Delaware

Every year between April and November, the waterfowl that live in the Bombay Hook National Wildlife Refuge are joined by a multitude of migratory birds. The refuge's salt marshes, swamps and freshwater pools are an essential link in the Great Atlantic Flyway, a chain of refuges stretching from the Gulf of Mexico to Canada.

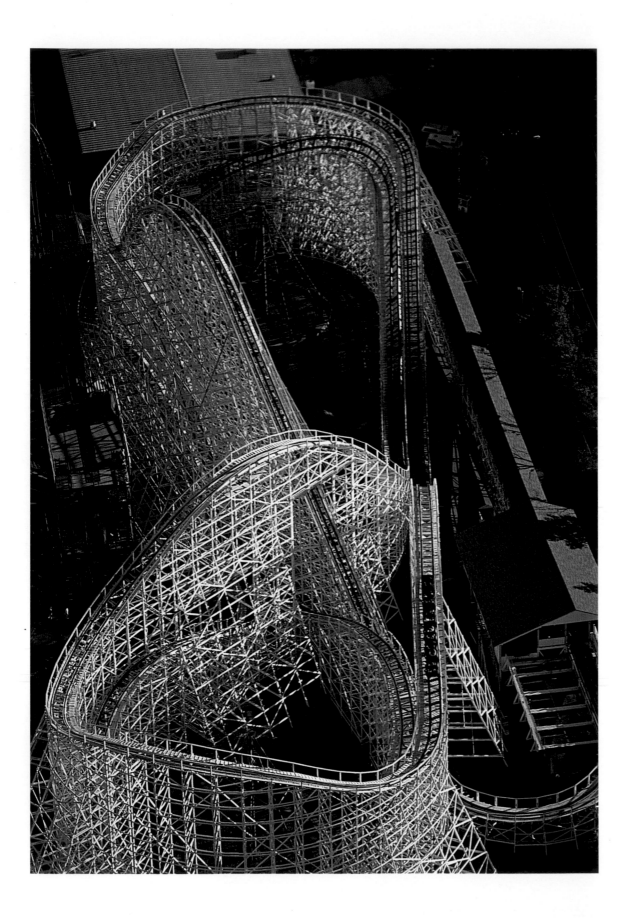

SPRINGFIELD, Massachusetts (left)

Summer revellers travel the ups and downs of the old rollercoaster at the Six Flags New England fun park in Agawam. The prototype for this rollercoaster was first shown at the 1939 World's Fair in New York. It provides a welcome diversion in the Springfield area, where relatively few tourists wander, despite such attractions as the Basketball Hall of Fame.

LAKES REGION, Maine (right)

The meandering character of Maine's coastline is repeated in the lakes region near the pristine wilderness of Baxter State Park in the north of the state. For 32 years, from 1939 to 1962, former governor Percival P. Baxter donated 202,064 acres of land surrounding Mount Katahdin to the state and people of Maine to ensure the land would be preserved for years to come.

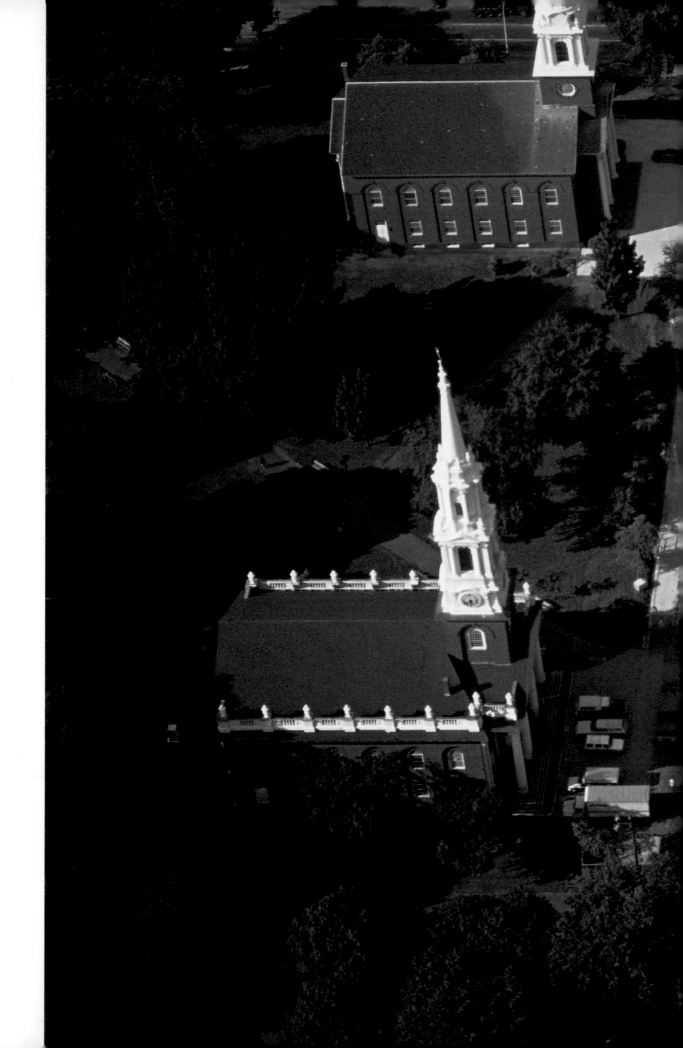

NEW HAVEN, Connecticut

Laid out in nine equal squares by the
Puritans in 1638, the New Haven Green
makes a fine place to gather for the
summer-long jazz festival and a bit of
sunbathing. The Puritans might find the
gathering somewhat wild, but Henry Ward
Beecher, who preached against slavery from
the steps of the United Congregational
Church (upper left) in 1855, would probably
advocate the freedom of all to choose.

AROOSTOOK COUNTY, Maine (left)

Over a million tons of potatoes are harvested each year in the fertile plains of Aroostook County in the northern tip of Maine. Until 1989, area schoolchildren were excused from classes to work the potato harvest, Maine's largest crop. Farmhouses in the north, such as this one, are often surrounded by vast stretches of forested wilderness.

ELLIS ISLAND, New Jersey (above)

Following a battle of pride between rivalling states, in 1998 the Supreme Court ruled that Ellis Island in New York Bay falls within the borders of New Jersey. More than 16 million immigrants made their first steps on American soil at the historic processing center, from 1892 until its closure in 1954. Today the center has been converted into a museum.

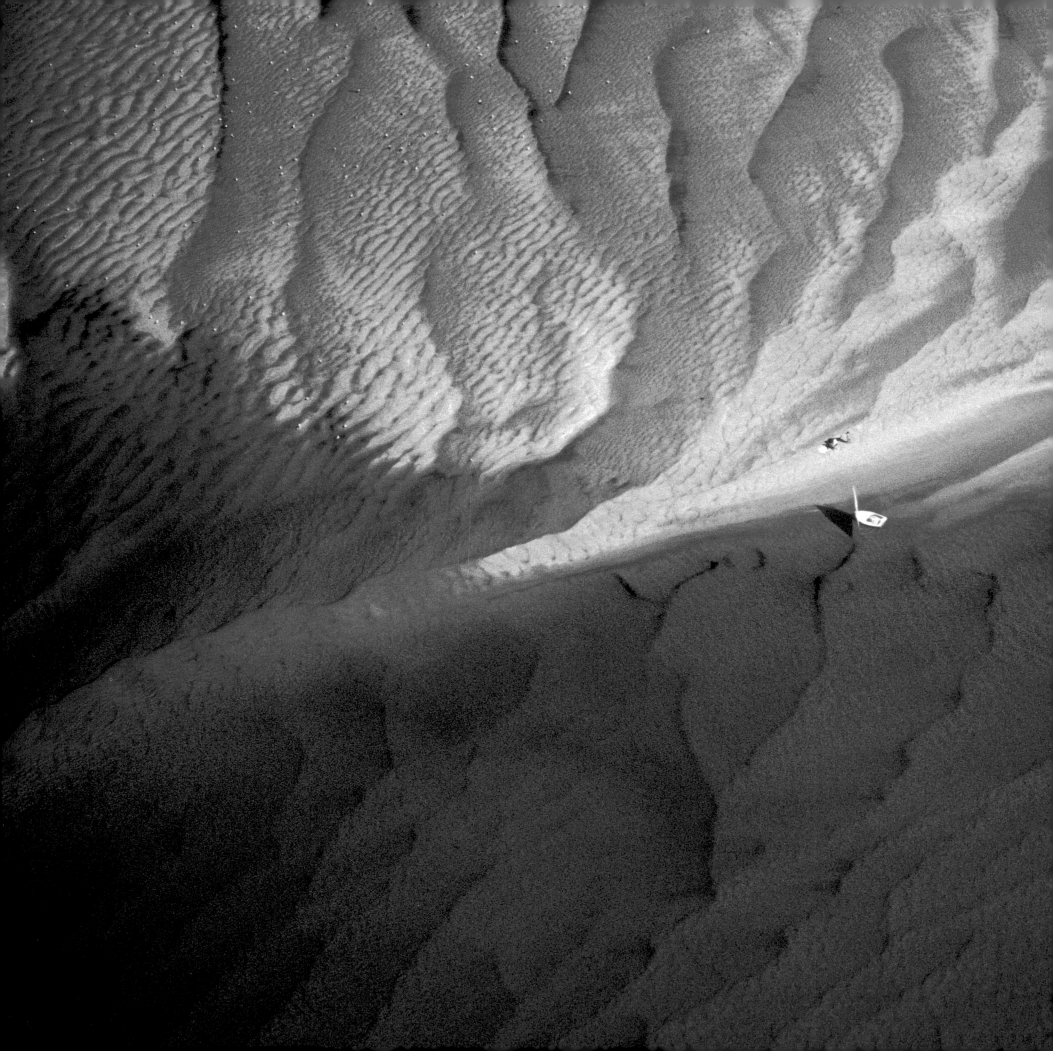

CAPE COD, Massachusetts

The patterns revealing the origins of Cape
Cod are as visible today as they were
11,000 years ago when the glaciers of the
last Ice Age retreated southward, pushing
with them the tons of sand and gravel that
became the 65-mile-long-Cape. The mighty
Gulf Stream that washes the coast north
of here changes direction off the Cape,
leaving in its wake a sea of shoals and
shifting sand pits.

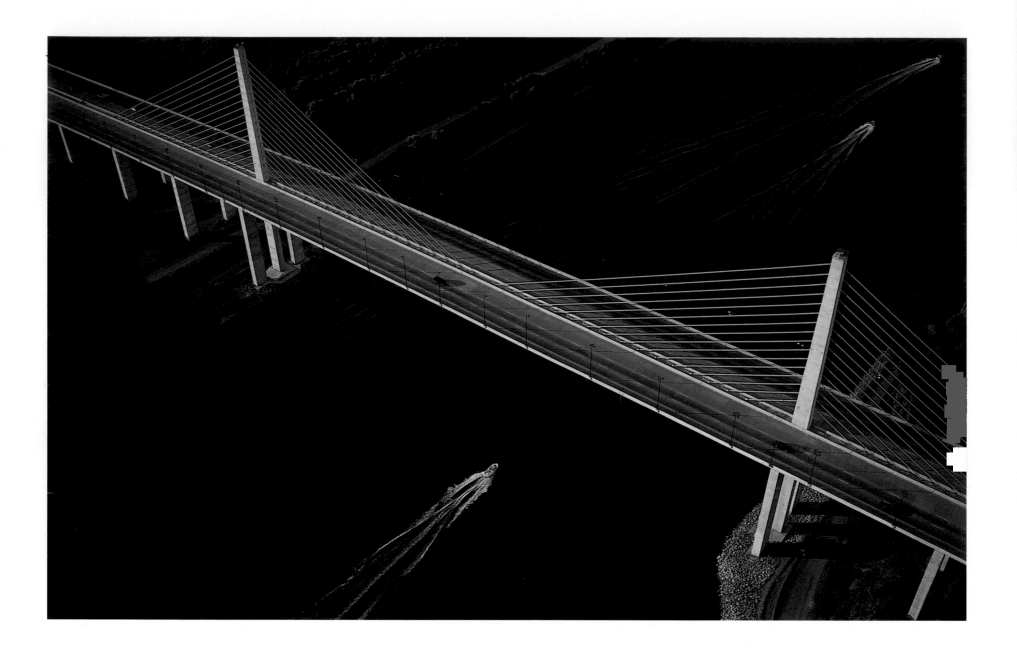

DELAWARE CANAL, Delaware (above)

The Delaware and Chesapeake Canal, constructed in 1829, flows west-to-east across Delaware, connecting Chesapeake Bay to the Atlantic. By providing an economical means of transport for the anthracite coal of the Upper Lehigh Valley to the eastern seaboard, the canal proved vital in supporting local industry during the 1800s.

HARRISVILLE, New Hampshire (right)

The traditional New England winter sport of ice fishing is especially popular on New Hampshire's many lakes. Shacks or "bobhouses" bearing their owners' names and addresses dot the ice. As well as providing shelter from the wind, they serve as focal points for families and friends to gather around fires and share thermoses of hot drinks.

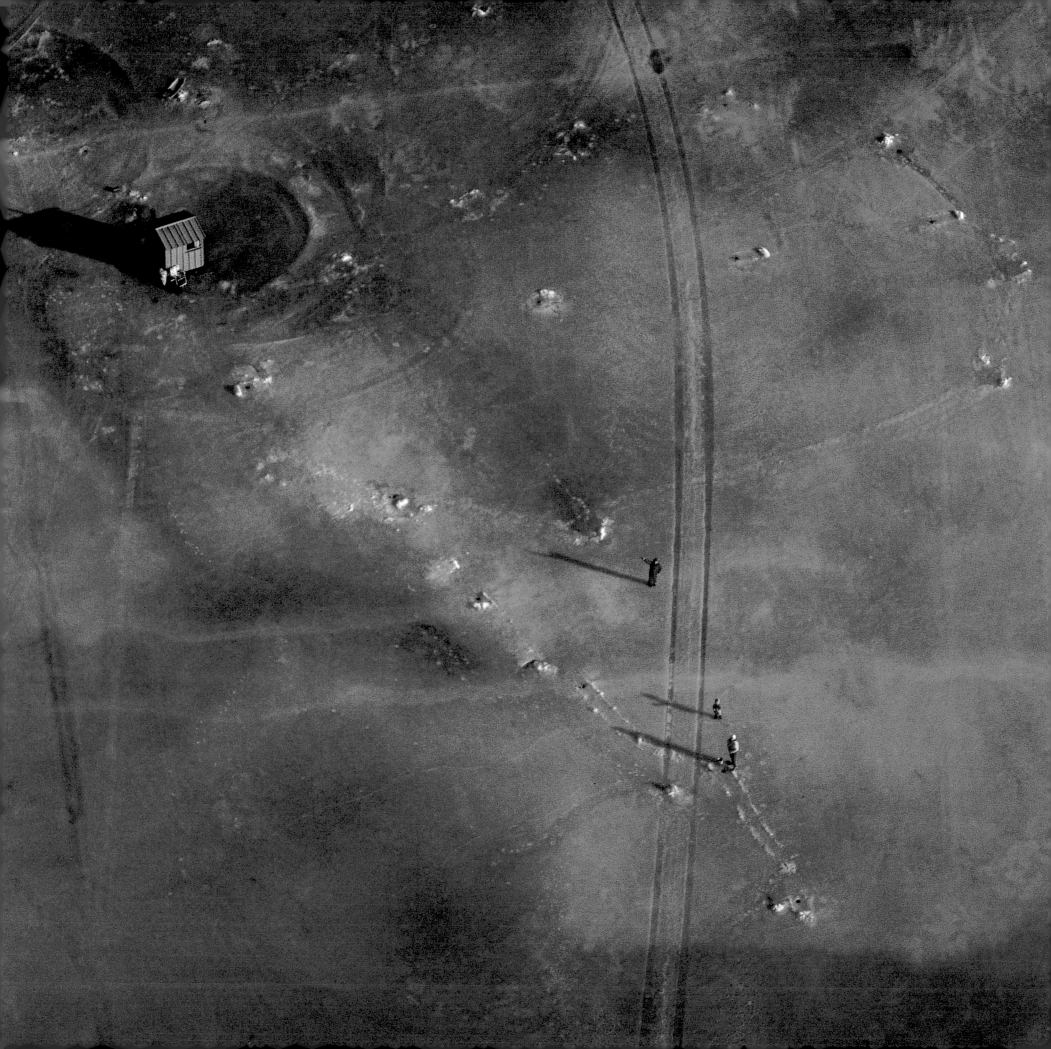

OXFORD, Connecticut

Ice floes choke a river near the small town
of Oxford, in southwestern Connecticut.
Nestled between the Housatonic and
Naugatuck rivers, Oxford's rural population
reside a stone's throw away from the
centers of Bridgeport and New Haven.
While winters can be bitterly cold, the
proximity of Connecticut to New York has
made it a sought-after area for those who
are attracted to the state's rural ambience
but do not desire to relinquish the
cosmopolitan pleasures of the city.

LIBERTY ISLAND, New York (left)

A gift from France to the United States, the statue officially known as "Liberty Enlightening the World" has become a global icon since she began greeting immigrants and visitors to New York in 1886. Visitors willing to endure the usually long waits can climb an elevator and stairs to the crown of the 151-foot-high structure, and are rewarded with panoramic views of New York.

SHELBURNE FARMS, Vermont (right)

The velvet grounds of Shelburne Farms wend around the shores of Lake Champlain. Built in the 1890s by railroad magnate Samuel Webb, Shelburne once incorporated over 4,000 acres, including a 110-room farmhouse, gatekeeper's house, several barns and houses for farm employees. Today the property—reduced to 1,000 acres—is an educational center and museum.

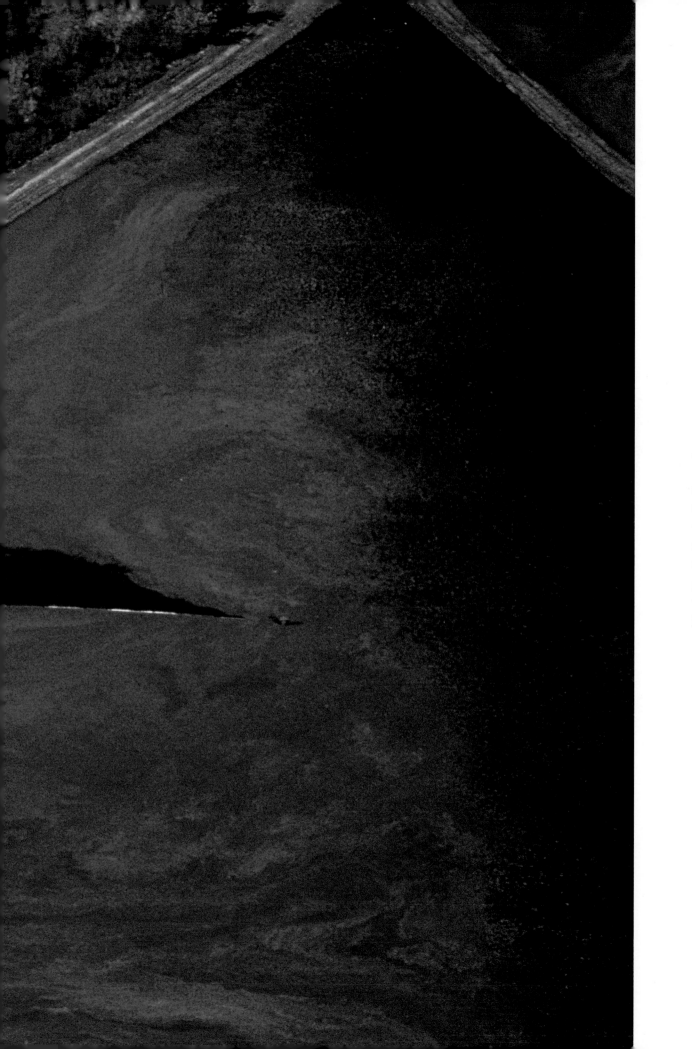

PLYMOUTH COUNTY, Massachusetts

A red sea of cranberries colors a bog near Lakeville. Such bogs are put to use in the cranberry industry, centered in Plymouth County. Set off by the blaze of autumn foliage, nearly 12,000 acres are harvested each year. When the scarlet berries are ripe, the bogs are flooded and the berries picked from the vine by a sort of floating thresher. Most of them are processed into juices, relishes or other cranberry products.

LITCHFIELD COUNTY,
Connecticut (left)

New England overall is not very well suited
to farming because of the poor soil quality
and short growing seasons. But some areas,
such as Connecticut's various river valleys,
nevertheless support at least small-scale
farming activity, as these silos near Kent
in the northwest of Connecticut can attest.

PROVIDENCE, Rhode Island (right)

The capital of Rhode Island, Providence
was founded in 1636 and maintains a
well-developed sense of its history. The
compact but lively city went into decline
in the middle of the twentieth century as
its manufacturing base dwindled. Since
then, it has renovated its downtown and
redeveloped its riverfront.

CAMBRIDGE, Massachusetts

Harvard University found its earthly origins
on the spacious plain of New Towne, a
farming hamlet later renamed Cambridge.
The universities of New England have been
critical to the region's life since 1636, the
year Harvard was founded as America's
first institution of higher learning. In this
image, the athletics fields can be seen
across the Charles River from the John
F. Kennedy School of Government.

NEW YORK CITY, New York (left)

The gray concrete metropolis of New York City can be seen here extending along the eastern edge of the Hudson River, at center, and the islands of Manhattan and Long Island (upper and center right). Across the Hudson to the west and south lies Newark, New Jersey. With 8 million people New York City is America's largest, although the green vegetation of the surrounding areas belies its urban nature.

WHITE MOUNTAINS,
New Hampshire (right)

Warm days and cold nights produce the best display of color in the autumn woods of the White Mountains. These are a small part of the Appalachian Mountains, which stretch for 1,500 miles from Quebec to Alabama. The pigments that "appear" on the leaves in fall are made visible by the breakdown of the dominant green chlorophyll.

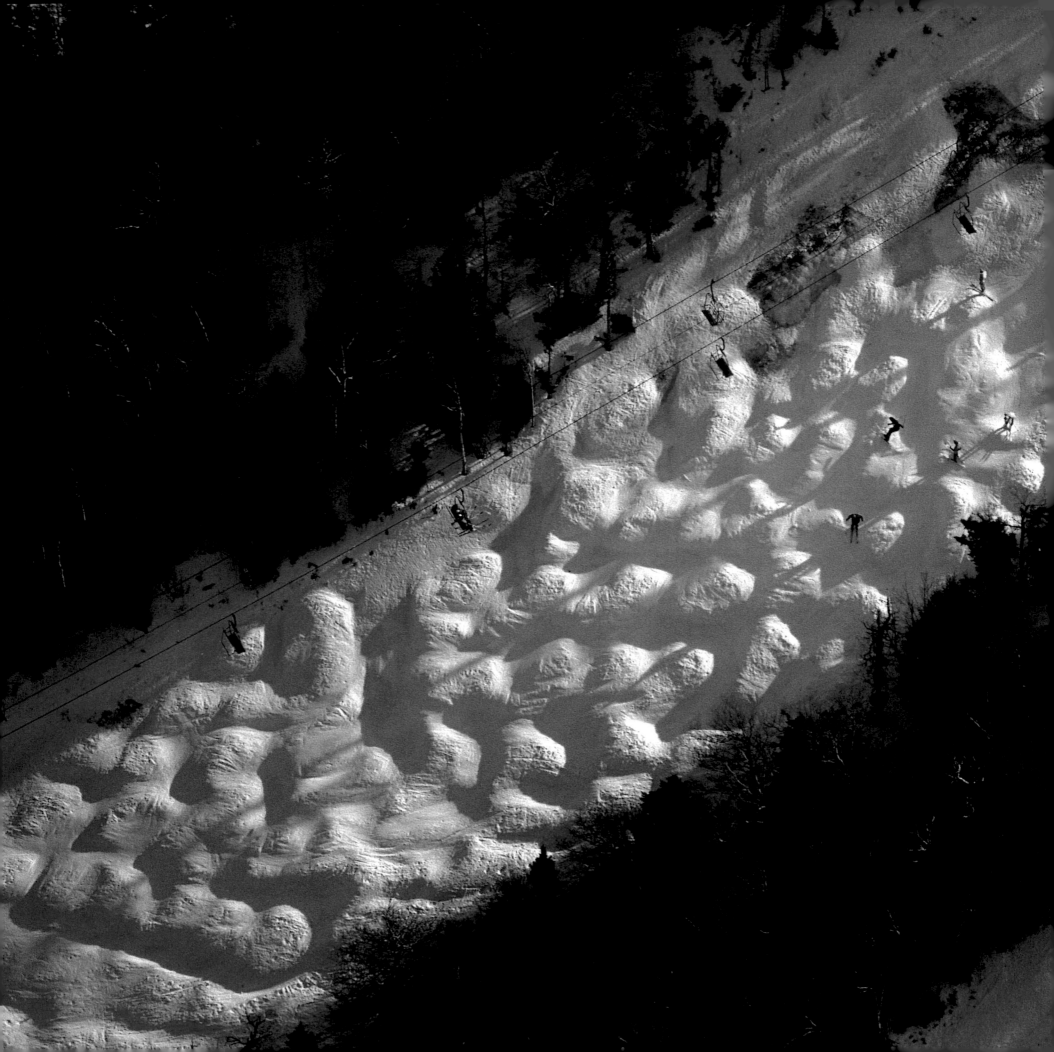

MOUNT SNOW, Vermont

Vermont's evergreen-forested mountains
draw winter sports fans from throughout
the region. Mount Snow, in the southern
part of the state, is one of the more
popular family ski areas. So named for
Reuben Snow, the farmer who originally
owned the land, the resort opened in 1954
with seven trails extending only halfway up
the mountain. Today, Mount Snow boasts
127 trails and 24 lifts.

WHITE MOUNTAINS, New Hampshire (above)

Monuments of strength and lofty achievement, like the statesmen they were named for, the Presidential Range is often called the "Ridgepole of New England." Story has it that a legendary climber, Ethan Allen Crawford, stood with seven friends on the summit of Mount Washington (above) and named the Presidential peaks with cheers and toasts of rum.

LITTLE COMPTON, Rhode Island (right)

A yellow Seaman biplane soars over the woodland that intersects the compact farms of Little Compton, one of the few areas in Rhode Island where farming is still the mainstay. Part of the Plymouth Colony until 1746, Little Compton is the birthplace of the Rhode Island Red, a breed of fowl that is the state bird of Rhode Island.

THE MID-ATLANTIC AND SOUTH

ALABAMA ❧ ARKANSAS ❧ FLORIDA ❧ GEORGIA ❧ KENTUCKY
LOUISIANA ❧ MARYLAND ❧ MISSISSIPPI ❧ NORTH CAROLINA
SOUTH CAROLINA ❧ TENNESSEE ❧ VIRGINIA
WASHINGTON D.C. ❧ WEST VIRGINIA

This region's differences with the rest of the country were once great enough almost to rend the nation apart. Resentments built up and finally spilled over into a full-scale Civil War between the northern and southern states in the 1860s. At the crux of the bloody four-year-long conflict was whether or not the "Southern" way of life—underpinned by slave labor and the plantation system of agriculture—should endure.

The country's first English colonists settled in Jamestown, Virginia, in 1607. They quickly recognized the agricultural potential of the southern coastal plains, which enjoyed long, hot summers, plenty of rain and mild winters. The settlers soon began cultivating tobacco, rice and indigo. But the crop that most strongly defined and shaped the region was cotton, for a whole system of social beliefs developed to justify the use of slave labor in its production.

Losing the struggle to secede from the Union made the Confederate states—Virginia, North Carolina, South Carolina, Arkansas, Tennessee, Mississippi, Florida,

WASHINGTON, District of Columbia

The nation's capital is dotted with monuments to presidents, war heroes and other notable Americans. Two of the most prominent landmarks, the Jefferson Memorial and the 555-foot-high Washington Monument, face each other across the Tidal Basin. Visitors can ride an elevator to an observation deck near the top of Washington's highest structure for panoramic views of the city.

Alabama, Georgia and Louisiana, as well as Texas—more defiantly inward-looking. The remainder of the South—Kentucky, Maryland, West Virginia and the District of Columbia, the nation's capital—had sided with the anti-slavery, more industrialized Union but identified strongly (especially in the case of the slave-owning Kentucky and Maryland) with the South. The region's isolationism impeded economic growth for many decades after the war. It also helped preserve the South's distinctive cultural traits.

Southerners, to some degree, still define themselves through their hospitality, colorful language and drawling accents, love of country, rhythm and blues music, strong sense of place, high church attendance and conservatism. Generations of African slaves have also left their mark on the region's diet, language and music. Change comes slowly here: Confederate flags still decorate more than a few pick-up trucks, and the "war between the states" is discussed as though it just recently ended.

Yet even as economic factors once drove the region to secede, so they have also brought it closer in line with the rest of the nation. The South's agricultural base and overall economy have both diversified in recent years. One of the biggest economic success stories in the so-called Sunbelt has been Atlanta, Georgia, a booming corporate nexus that has promoted itself as "too busy to hate." Further south, locals like to quip that Florida—a one-time Spanish colony whose largest city, Miami, now hums with Cuban culture—has grown rich on tourism, farming and drug smuggling. Its warm climate, beaches and laid-back lifestyle have helped make it popular with retirees and wintering northerners. Miami has also exploited its location and its large Spanish-speaking population to become a center for trade with Latin America.

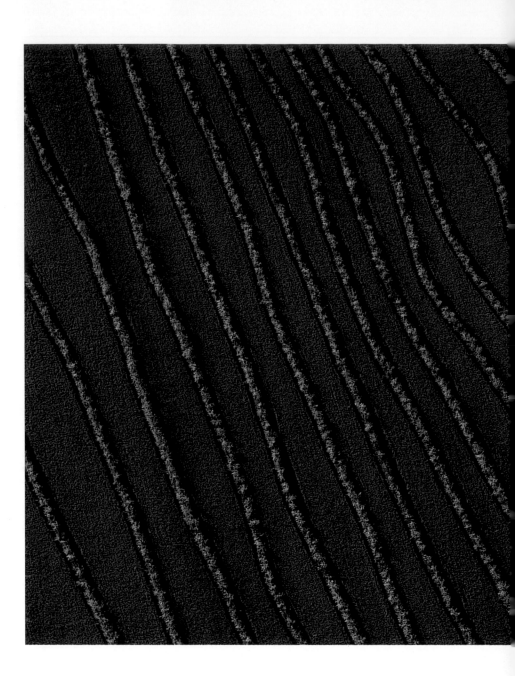

RICE FIELDS, Arkansas (above)

The hot, fertile South is no longer a continuous Cotton Belt spanning from the Atlantic Ocean to Texas. The region's agricultural base now comprises a wide variety of crops. For example, rice fields, such as this one in Arkansas, are irrigated in the Gulf Coast Plain region and Mississippi bottomlands.

FLORIDA KEYS, Florida (right)

A chain of sprawling islands, often barely distinguishable from the sea—these are the Florida Keys, joined to the mainland by the Overseas Highway, which follows the sun to Key West. Tropical by climate and inclination, relatively isolated from the mainland, the Keys offer a way of life unique in the United States.

ATCHAFALAYA BASIN, Louisiana

The Atchafalaya Basin cuts a 15-mile-wide path along southern Louisiana. Teeming with alligators and more than 300 species of birds, the 860,000-acre basin boasts one of the country's largest remaining river-basin swamps. Its abundant cypress trees have been an important resource to the area's settlers for hundreds of years.

ATLANTA, Georgia (left)

In the 1830s, Atlanta was nothing more than a railroad hub named "Terminus;" now the booming metropolis of more than 3 million is one of the nation's fastest growing cities. A transportation and communications center for the nation's southeast, it is home to world-famous companies such as Coca-Cola. But expansion has come at the price of sprawl and a strained road infrastructure.

FORT LAUDERDALE, Florida (right)

An early arrival stakes out a cabana from the orderly rows lining the beach with military precision at Fort Lauderdale. Once known as the capital of spring break, the city has in recent years discouraged the collegiate practitioners of that yearly rite and cultivated a more stolid image as a respectable family vacation spot.

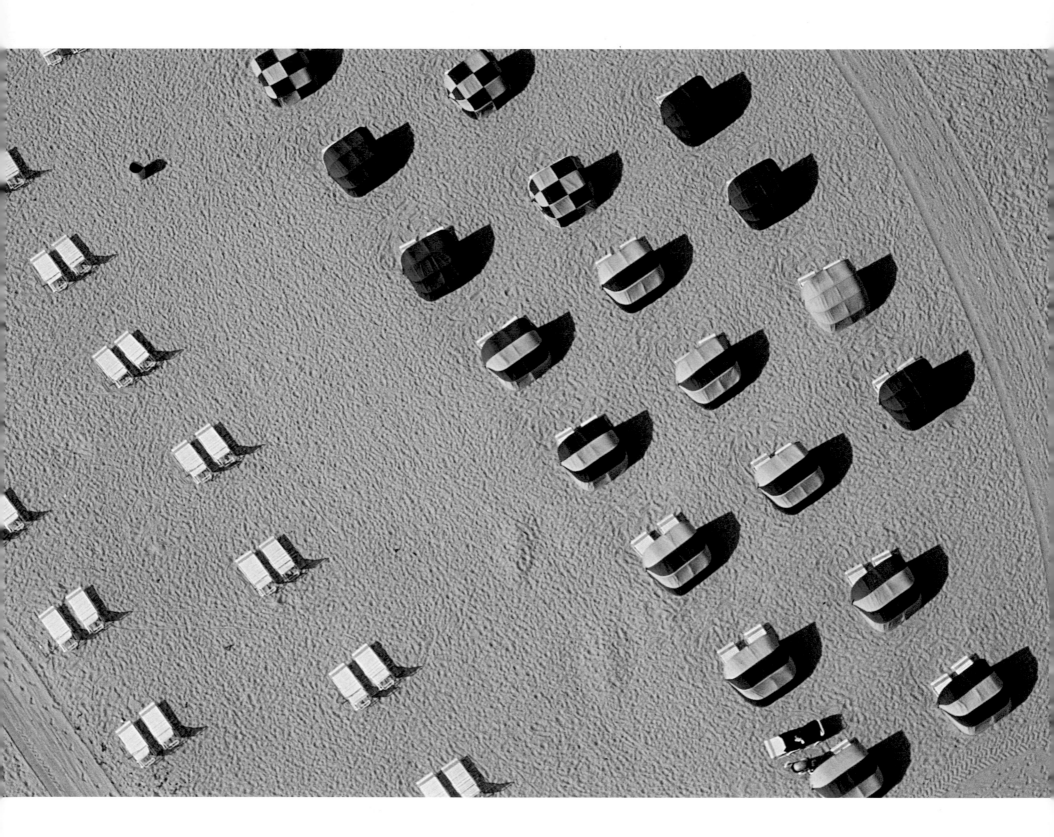

THE MID-ATLANTIC AND SOUTH

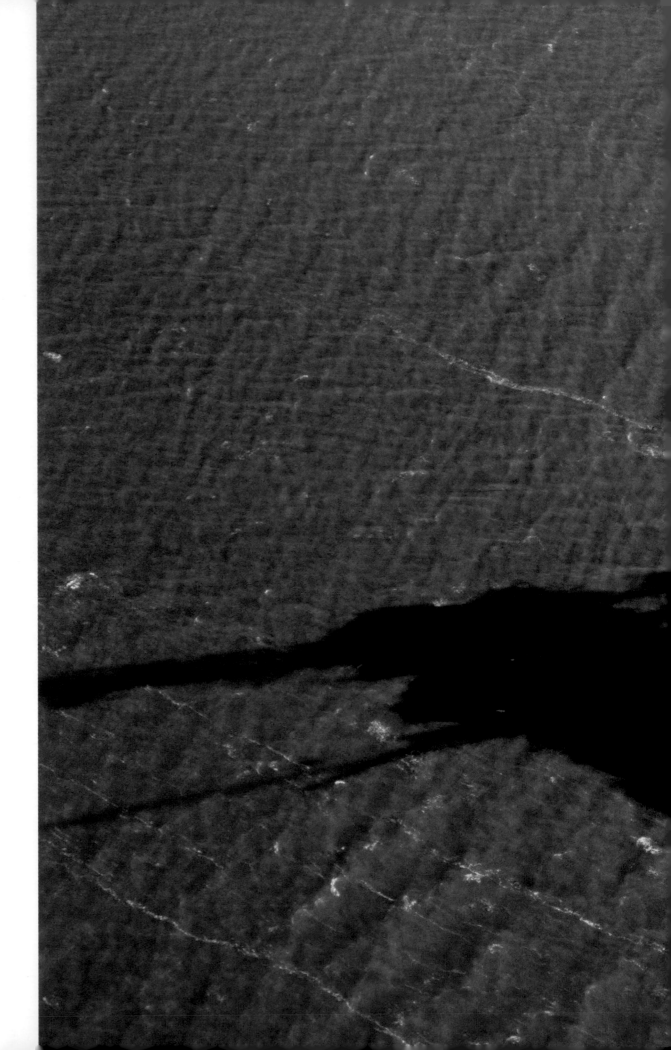

MOBILE BAY, Alabama

Oil rigs, such as this one being constructed off the coast of Alabama, extract the petroleum deposits that lie on the North American continental shelf, which extends underwater dozens of miles beyond the coastline. The oil industry is an important component of the Alabama economy.

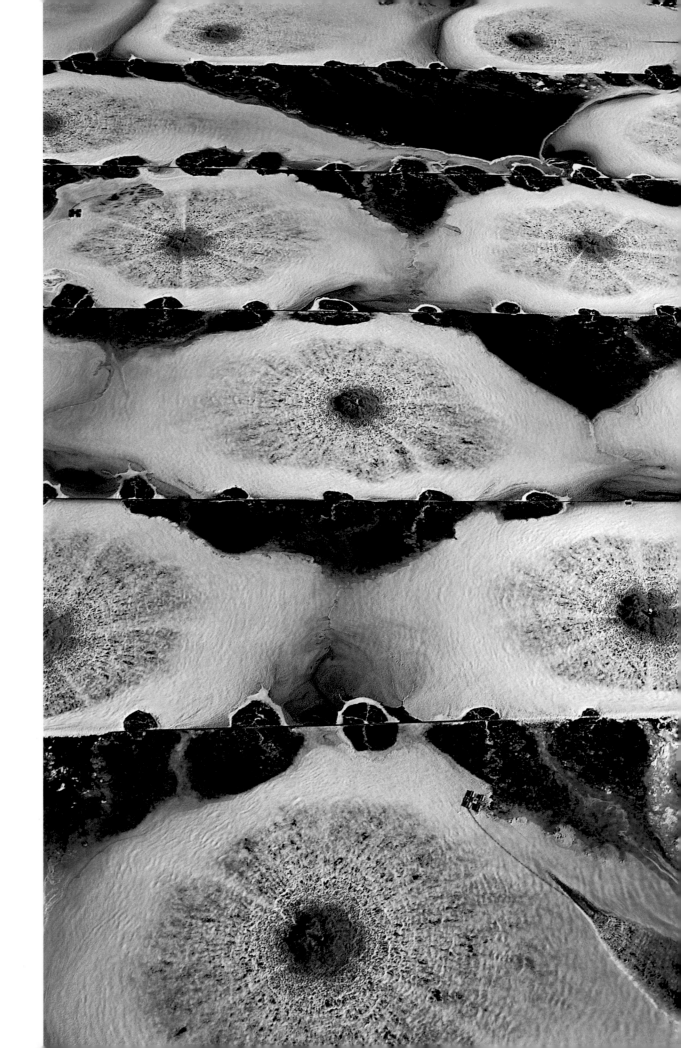

KEY WEST, Florida (left)

The Magic Carpet miniature golf course
at Key West sports a nautical theme in
keeping with the island city's history.
A century ago, Key West, more than
150 miles southwest of the mainland, was
one of the richest cities per capita in the
United States, its 17,000 residents engaged
in fishing, sponging and salvaging ships
and cargos off the Florida reef. Today this
multifaceted city is a naval base, tourist
destination and fishing town.

CHARLESTON COUNTY,
South Carolina (right)

Seen directly from above at a height of
100 feet, the aeration ponds of wood pulp
mills have the beauty of sea anemones.
However, the sulfate process of turning
wood chips into pulp has an earthier
by-product: a smell not unlike rotten eggs.
Ponds such as this one near Charleston,
South Carolina, are designed to clean the
wastewater of the plant.

WASHINGTON, District of Columbia

Washington's Library of Congress, spread across three buildings, is the nation's premier research library. Only a quarter of the 115 million items in its collection are books; the rest include films, photographs, music recordings, maps, prints and manuscripts. The mahogany desks in the Jefferson Building's Main Reading Room are available to all researchers.

ANNAPOLIS, Maryland (left)

With the excitement of the Chesapeake Bay Schooner Race as a backdrop, the tranquil white domed steeple of the Maryland State House, at center, highlights the structure from surrounding downtown Annapolis. It is the oldest state capitol still in continuous legislative use, and has been a National Historic Landmark since 1968.

ARLINGTON, Virginia (right)

One of the nation's most important memorial sites, Arlington National Cemetery lies in Arlington, Virginia, just across the Potomac River from the District of Columbia. More than 150,000 veterans' graves line its rolling hills. The most visited memorials are those of John F. Kennedy and Robert F. Kennedy and the Tomb of the Unknowns.

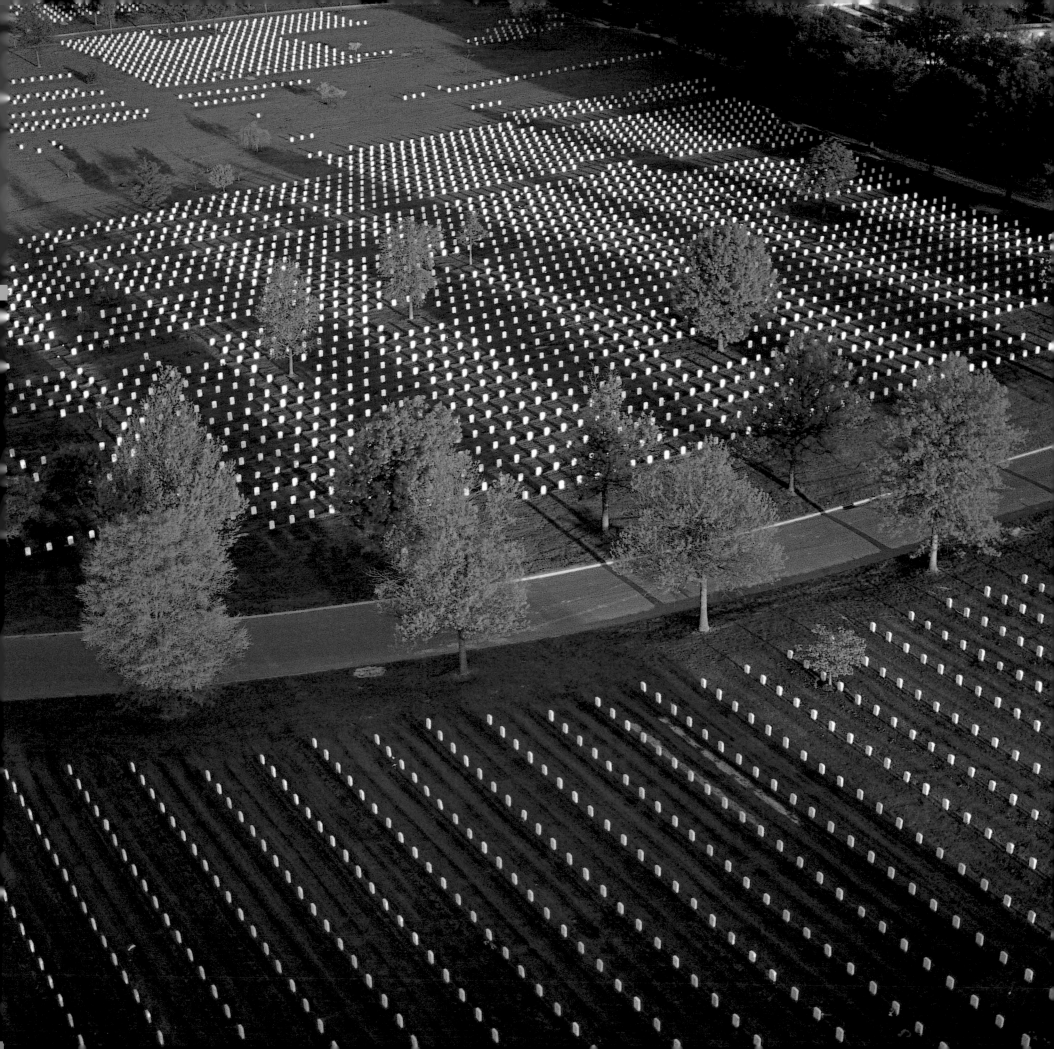

BISCAYNE BAY NATIONAL PARK,
Florida

"Stiltsville," an historic collection of
vacation homes perched just above the
seagrass beds of Biscayne Bay, was first built
in the 1930s. Today the seven remaining
structures, accessible only by sea, are no
longer privately owned but are under the
direction of the National Park Service. A
rehabilitation process is currently underway
to make these South Florida landmarks safe
for community use, although their final
purpose is still undecided.

LOUISVILLE, Kentucky (left)

The bustling river port city of Louisville was named after France's King Louis XVI, in gratitude for his country's help in America's War of Independence. Thanks to its central position in the eastern United States, the city has drawn many immigrants from throughout Europe.

CHEROKEE INDIAN RESERVATION, North Carolina (above)

Mist and dusk caress the hills of the Cherokee Indian Reservation. The reservation is populated by descendants of the Cherokee who managed to avoid the American government's forced relocation of their tribe to Oklahoma along the "Trail of Tears" in the mid-1800s.

CHESAPEAKE BAY, Maryland

The Chesapeake Bay Bridge is often choked with traffic on warm-weather weekends, as residents of Washington, D.C. escape for a few days to Maryland's laid-back Eastern Shore, with its small and rustic towns, inns, lighthouses and farmland. The bridge crosses Kent Island, the largest island in the 195-mile-long estuary famous for its fishing "watermen."

WASHINGTON, District of
Columbia (left)

The starkly modern INTELSAT headquarters
building offers a sharp contrast to the
neoclassical official buildings usually
associated with Washington, D.C. It was
designed for maximum energy efficiency,
the glass structure allowing for natural
light to filter in to the offices within.

MISSISSIPPI RIVER,
Mississippi (right)

Seen through a thermal emission and
reflection lens, the shifting sediments of the
Mississippi Delta are clearly distinguishable
as green, contrasting with the pale blue
land and darker blue waters of the Gulf of
Mexico, at lower left. While the main
shipping channel runs straight through to
the sea, the majority of channels in the
delta are constantly forming and silting up.

VENICE, Florida (left)

Modular homes radiate a central recreation hall in Venice, on the
Gulf Coast of Florida. The pool and shuffleboard courts are the focus
of these communities, which provide affordable housing for thousands
of the state's new residents. With approximately one-third of the
current population over the age of 65, the Gulf Coast, with its
temperate climate and slow pace of life, is one of the country's more
favored retirement destinations.

WACCASASSA BAY PRESERVE STATE PARK, Florida (above)

Cabbage palm hammocks rise from the floodplain marshes of the
twisting Waccasassa River, one of the most remote areas in Florida.
These marshes are transitional zones, where fresh and salt water mix,
and the division between land and sea gradually blurs as the river
meanders to the Gulf of Mexico. The hammock preserved here is a
remnant of the vast stretches of forest, known as the Gulf Hammock,
that once covered Florida.

WASHINGTON, District of
Columbia (left)

The Archives-Navy Memorial is one of the
stops in Washington, D.C.'s extensive subway
system, which opened in the mid-1970s.
The memorial plaza, which features a large
granite map of the world, honors the men
and women who sail the globe in the
service of the United States Navy. It is also
a popular venue for military band concerts.

BUFFALO NATIONAL RIVER,
Arkansas (right)

Arkansas' Buffalo National River became
the first federally protected river in 1972.
Flowing among limestone bluffs along the
course of an ancient riverbed, it offers
canoeing, whitewater rafting, hiking,
fishing and historical sightseeing, in
three wilderness areas and 135 miles of
the 150-mile-long Buffalo River.

KEY WEST, Florida (above)

Any bit of solid surface, even a gutted wreck, is sufficient for a bold red mangrove to set down roots and begin the laborious process of island building. While Key West was a wrecker's bazaar in the nineteenth century, wrecking fell into decline around the turn of the century, as lighthouses were constructed and ships turned to steam and steel.

SMITH ISLAND, Maryland (right)

Named for Captain John Smith, who explored the Chesapeake Bay area in the seventeenth century, the three-island group known as Smith Island settles in for another isolated winter. Smith Island is the only inhabited island group in Chesapeake Bay, and, while accessible only by boat, it is becoming a tourist destination during the crabbing season.

NORTHERN PANHANDLE,
West Virginia (left)

Trees hug the fence-lines surrounding the whitewashed buildings of a hilltop farm in the Northern Panhandle region of West Virginia. As the name suggests, the Northern Panhandle is a narrow strip of land along the Ohio River that juts into neighboring Pennsylvania and Ohio.

GREAT SMOKY MOUNTAINS
Tennessee (right)

The area surrounding Knoxville, in eastern Tennessee, is interlaced by rivers that flow in and around the foothills of the Great Smoky Mountains. Further south from here is the Great Smoky Mountains National Park, which is world-renowned for the diversity of its flora and fauna.

THE GREAT LAKE STATES

ILLINOIS ∾ INDIANA ∾ MICHIGAN
MINNESOTA ∾ OHIO ∾ WISCONSIN

The central Great Lake states have benefited greatly from their proximity to the five vast bodies of water that help define the United States–Canada border. Comprising one of the world's most extensive inland waterway systems, the lakes were long ago recognized as a convenient route along which to transport people and goods between North America's interior and its eastern seaboard, from where they could be shipped to far-flung ports across the ocean.

Beaver fur was an early resource to be exported in this way. France, which claimed the area until being forced to yield it to Britain in the mid-1700s, established a series of forts to secure its position and serve its *voyageurs*, who plied the waterways in fur-laden canoes.

After the area stretching from the established colonies west to the Mississippi River was ceded to the United States following the War of Independence, settlers in search of more fertile farmland began streaming in from New England, Kentucky and Tennessee. The flat or gently rolling land in the southern sections remains heavily agricultural to this day, although large, mechanized holdings have for the most part supplanted family farms. The region's colder northern sections remain more sparsely

CHICAGO, Illinois

A Chicago landmark and one of the city's top tourist destinations, Navy Pier was opened in 1916 as a combined shipping and recreation facility. After falling into disuse for much of the 1970s and 1980s, it was given a facelift and reopened in 1995 as a complex of shops, restaurants, exhibition facilities and various other attractions.

populated. But their clear lakes and coniferous woods, roamed by wildlife such as moose and timber wolves, make them popular with vacationers.

Most of the region's residents make their homes in towns or cities. Some urban centers have their roots in forts the French erected at important waterway junctions. With the arrival of the railroads, Chicago, Illinois, now the nation's third-largest city, became an important hub and meatpacking center catering to midwest cattle ranchers wanting to sell their product to eastern markets. Other lake port cities became convenient way-stations for iron ore shipments from mines in northern Wisconsin, Minnesota and Michigan.

To the rest of the nation, the Great Lake states represent "America": a land of white bread, apple pie, and well-tended farms and suburbs. No wonder then that companies like to test-market new products in Ohio, and political strategists ask themselves if something "will play in Peoria," with the residents of a medium-sized Illinois town acting as stand-ins for America as a whole.

LAKE SUPERIOR, Minnesota (left)

For seamen and fishermen in trouble in
storms and fog, the octagonal Split Rock
lighthouse cast its beacon for nearly
60 years. Radar eventually made it obsolete,
but it stands repainted and restored on
Lake Superior's north shore. It stands atop
a palisade, overlooking waters so lethal in
storm that scores of large vessels, many
of them freighters hundreds of feet long,
lie at the bottom of Lake Superior.

FARMLAND, Wisconsin (right)

Green fields and golden soil create contour
lines of contrasting colors and textures,
echoing the undulating topography of
rural Wisconsin. Much of the state's once
heavily forested land is now used for
agriculture. The state is best known for its
dairies, but it also produces a significant
amount of corn, soybeans and other crops.

STRAITS OF MACKINAC, Michigan

The Round Island lighthouse began guiding boats through the Straits of Mackinac, between Lake Michigan and Lake Huron, in 1895. An automatic beacon eventually made the manned lighthouse obsolete. It is now an historic site that harks back to the days when sailing these waters was far more perilous than today.

HILL ANNEX MINE, Minnesota (left)

Stands of evergreens and the blue waters of a freshly born lake have transformed the ravaged earth of the abandoned pit of the Hill Annex Mine, in Calumet on the Mesabi Range, into a pleasing scene of nature reviving itself. When the pit was active, miners pumped out the spring water as they burrowed downward to remove the ore. Hill Annex operates now as a Minnesota state park.

THE GREAT LAKES, North America (right)

The Great Lakes, which divide the United States and Canada, include four of the 10 largest freshwater lakes in the world, and together hold 18 percent of the planet's fresh water. These waterways proved pivotal in the initial exploration of America and, with the construction of a system of canals, provided impetus to the industrial development of the nation.

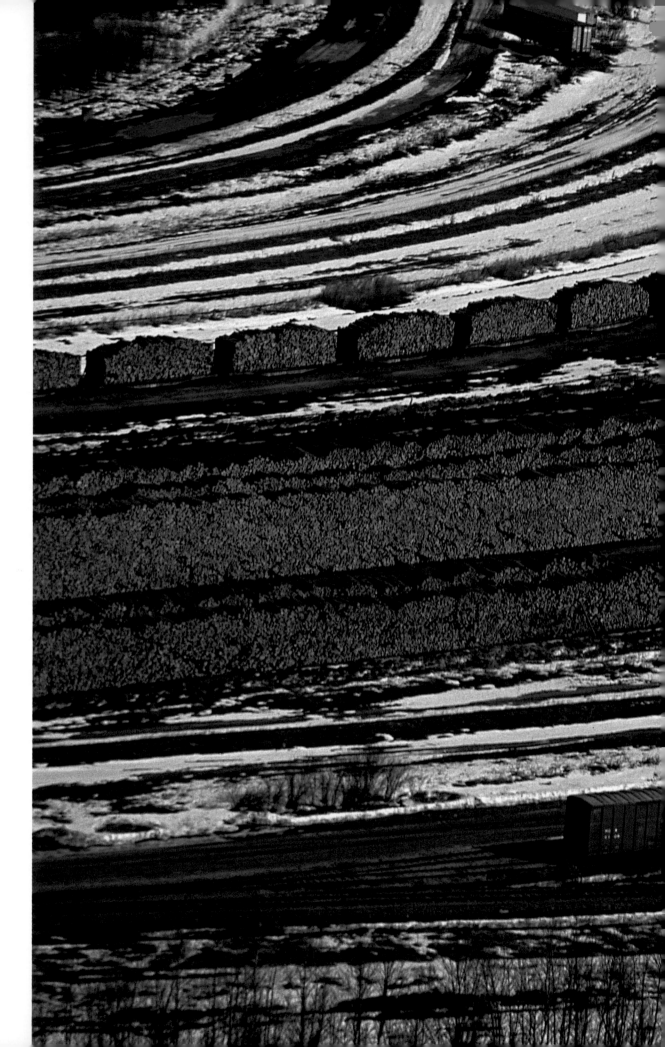

INTERNATIONAL FALLS, Minnesota

Thousands of logs are piled in the Boise
Cascade pulpwood yard at International
Falls, loaded on flatcars and hauled to the
mill a mile away. Logging was important
to Minnesota long before agriculture took
hold. Over time, logging camps developed
into towns, and towns into some of the
state's major cities.

LAKE SUPERIOR, Michigan (left)

The world's largest freshwater body of water, Lake Superior laps the banks of Michigan's Upper Peninsula. The largest, highest and deepest of the Great Lakes is also the least polluted. Its frigid waters have claimed the lives of many sailors whose ships were destroyed while attempting to cross the lake on foggy or stormy winter days.

INTERNATIONAL FALLS, Minnesota (right)

Vast stacks of spruce, birch and poplar logs trucked into International Falls await conversion into wood chips and ultimately into fine-quality office paper at the Boise Cascade paper mill. The paper mill is one of the town's largest employers.

PINE FORESTS, Michigan

Forest clearance in stands of pines such
as these helps promote new growth and
is part of a long-term wildlife incentive
program to create a better breeding habitat
for the Kirtland's warbler. This stocky gray
and yellow bird is one of the country's
rarest species, nesting only in the sparse
undergrowth of five- to six-year-old
jack-pine forests.

RED RIVER VALLEY, Minnesota (above)

A long voyage begins from the middle of North America, as soybeans from a Red River Valley field are loaded onto a truck for a destination that could be ultimately halfway around the world. A relatively recent phenomenon in American agriculture, half of Minnesota's soybean crop, grown on over 5 million acres, is shipped overseas.

COLUMBUS, Ohio (right)

The skyline of Columbus rises sharply from the gentle curves of the Scioto River. Founded in 1812, Columbus, the capital of Ohio and its most populous city, was an important river port from its early years. A series of canals and locks constructed along the Scioto River now give its varied industries access to the Gulf of Mexico.

LUVERNE, Minnesota

The sun shimmers off patches of frosted
farmland in the early morning fog. The flat
and fertile grainfields of northwestern
Minnesota were once a huge glacial lake,
Lake Agassiz. These rich soils have produced
food crops since the mid-nineteenth
century. Today, wheat, sugar beets,
potatoes, soybeans, flax and sunflowers
are the main produce.

MINNEAPOLIS, Minnesota (left)

The waning sun transforms downtown Minneapolis towers into stained glass. The Twin Cities of St. Paul and Minneapolis, separated by the generous curves of the Mississippi River, are bastions of commerce and industry in a state blessed with more than 10,000 lakes and wilderness areas.

OCOOCH MOUNTAINS, Wisconsin (right)

These fog-shrouded hills, forming part of the ancient Ocooch mountain range in southwest Wisconsin, are among the roughly 40 percent of the state's land area that remains forested, despite heavy exploitation by the lumber industry.

EVANSVILLE, Indiana (left)

Caught in silhouette, a barge makes its way down the Ohio River, near Evansville, Indiana. Industry such as coal, steel, plastics and car manufacturing are vital to the region's economy—the Ohio River has historically been a significant inland waterway for barge traffic, and has remained prominent despite the rise of interstate highways and air travel.

ST. PAUL, Minnesota (right)

The cathedral of St. Paul, built on the highest point of downtown St. Paul, overlooks the city's skyline. It was constructed in Renaissance style to emulate St. Peter's Basilica in Rome. The cornerstone was laid in 1907, with the cathedral opening in 1925. Its dome echoes that of the state capitol not far away.

PIPESTONE, Minnesota (left)

Indians quarried rock for their traditional peace pipes not far from the
town of Pipestone, which today is both city and interpreter of those years
and a showcase for them in the red rock of its more historic buildings.

MARYLAND, Ohio (above)

Ohio may be better known for its manufacturing, but the state's
economy also relies strongly on agriculture. Farmers take advantage of
its limestone-enriched soils to grow corn, soybeans and other crops.

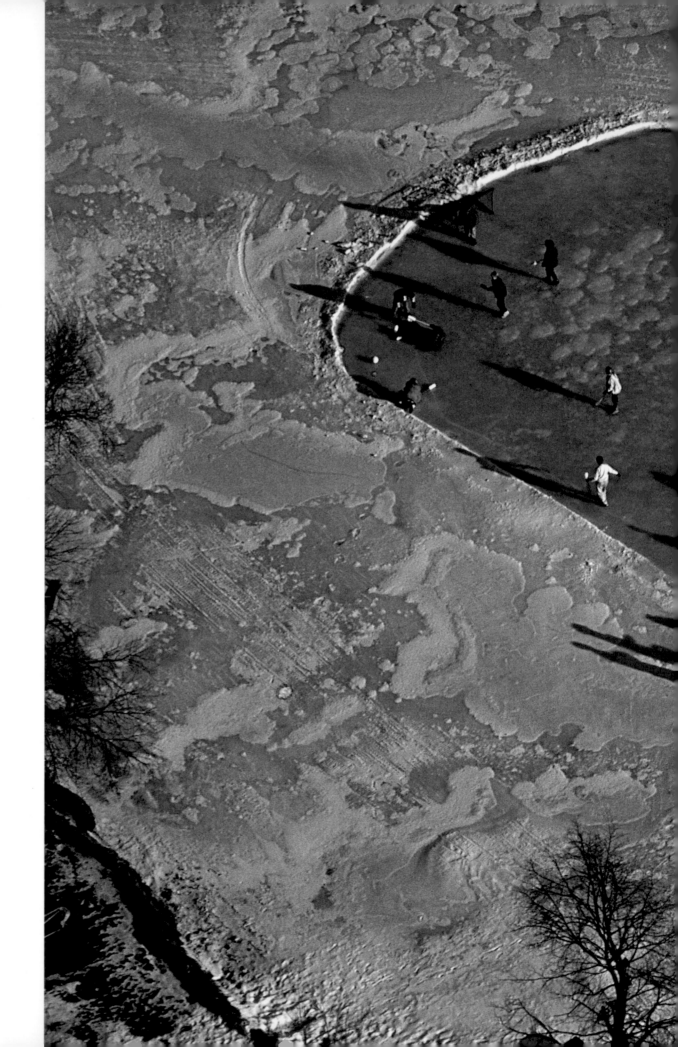

LAKE SHETEK, Minnesota

Fun and games take novel forms in farm
country in the middle of winter. Broomball
has not graduated to the Olympics, but it
makes a great Sunday afternoon recreation
on Lake Shetek. Players advance the ball
with brooms whose bristles are sawed short
for better control. On this rink, geography
can be tricky. If you hit the ball out of
bounds and there's a wind, you may have
to chase it down the lake for half a mile.

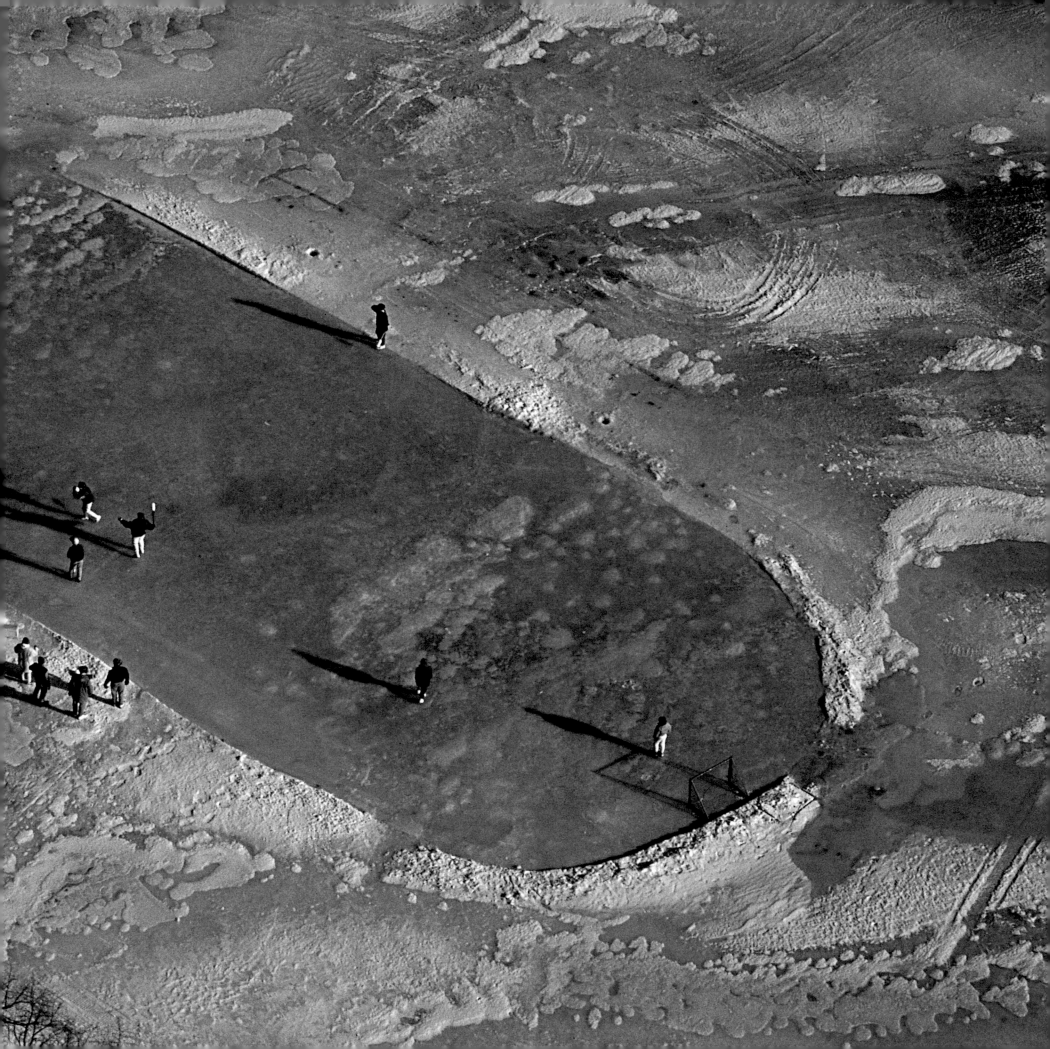

LAKE SUPERIOR, Minnesota (left)

A windsurfer on Lake Superior braves 40-mile-an-hour winds and waves up to 10 feet high. In storm, huge crests of whitewater explode against the cliffs and ledges of some of the oldest rocks on Earth. At other times the lake is serene, seemingly introspective. Aquatic sports are limited because of the lake's cold water.

CINCINNATI, Ohio (right)

Cincinnati, the third-largest city in Ohio, is an important industrial, commercial and cultural center. It has a busy riverfront and suburbs that extend into neighboring Kentucky and Indiana. The Riverfront Stadium shown here—home to the Cincinnati Reds—was opened in 1970 and demolished at the end of 2002, to be replaced with the Great American Ball Park.

THE MOUNTAINS AND THE PLAINS

IDAHO ∽ IOWA ∽ KANSAS ∽ MISSOURI ∽ MONTANA
NEBRASKA ∽ NORTH DAKOTA ∽ OKLAHOMA
SOUTH DAKOTA ∽ WYOMING

A large part of the area now known as America's breadbasket—the Great Plains states of Iowa, Kansas, Missouri, Nebraska, the Dakotas and Oklahoma—was once dismissed as a "Great American Desert." So thought the explorers dispatched to survey the little-known territory. They reported that the poor soil and infrequent rainfall in much of the continent's vast interior lowland rendered it useless to all but the Native Americans who had hunted buffalo on its prairies for centuries.

This stark appraisal convinced many pioneers to settle west of the Rocky Mountains instead. Vast temperature changes between summer and winter, combined with blizzards, strong summer winds, tornadoes and hailstorms, were compelling reasons not to linger on the prairies. And the few trees, especially in the region's western expanses, made for a dearth of firewood and building materials.

Innovations such as mechanical well drills, coupled with hardier crop species, eventually overcame some of these obstacles and helped convince settlers to begin claiming the virtually free land in the 1860s. Wheat, corn and other crops gradually covered the prairies, until very little native grass remained.

BITTERROOT RANGE, Montana

Tethered to the mountaintop by steel cables able to withstand hundred-mile-an-hour winds, this lookout
in western Montana is devoted to detecting summer forest fires, rather than winter blizzards. Montana is
known as "big sky country," a name that evokes the majesty of its natural environment and dominance
of that environment over the effects of human impact.

Large tracts of the Great Plains have also been used for cattle ranching. The cowboy era, which saw herds of cattle herded from Texas up to freewheeling railroad towns in Kansas and Missouri, lasted only from the 1860s until the 1880s, but it came to symbolize the region and define the American "Wild West."

While the rural character of the plains has diminished as agri-businesses have replaced many family farms and prompted younger generations to pursue manufacturing or service industry jobs in the towns, the situation is far different in the Rocky Mountain states of Idaho, Montana

and Wyoming. Still among the country's most sparsely populated areas—Montana, for example, has about six people per square mile, which makes it a magnet for fringe groups, survivalists and loners—these states have been drawing many new part-year and permanent residents in recent years.

The still-plentiful tracts of unspoiled wilderness are now recognized as valuable for tourism. Rising majestically on the western fringe of the Great Plains, the snow-capped Rocky Mountains stretch from Alaska to the Mexican border. National parks such as Wyoming's Yellowstone draw millions of visitors eager to experience nature's grandeur.

HUTCHINSON, Kansas (left)

A sharp reminder of the continued importance of agricultural produce to the Midwest, the world's longest single grain tower dominates the flat landscape of the railyards at Hutchinson in central Kansas. With a population of about 40,000, Hutchinson is one of the state's important rural centers, and has been the home of the Kansas State Fair since 1913.

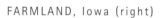
FARMLAND, Iowa (right)

Iowa can claim some of the world's most fertile agricultural land and is the country's leader in corn and soybean production. Yet, despite its agrarian image, today industry rather than farming generates the most income for the state.

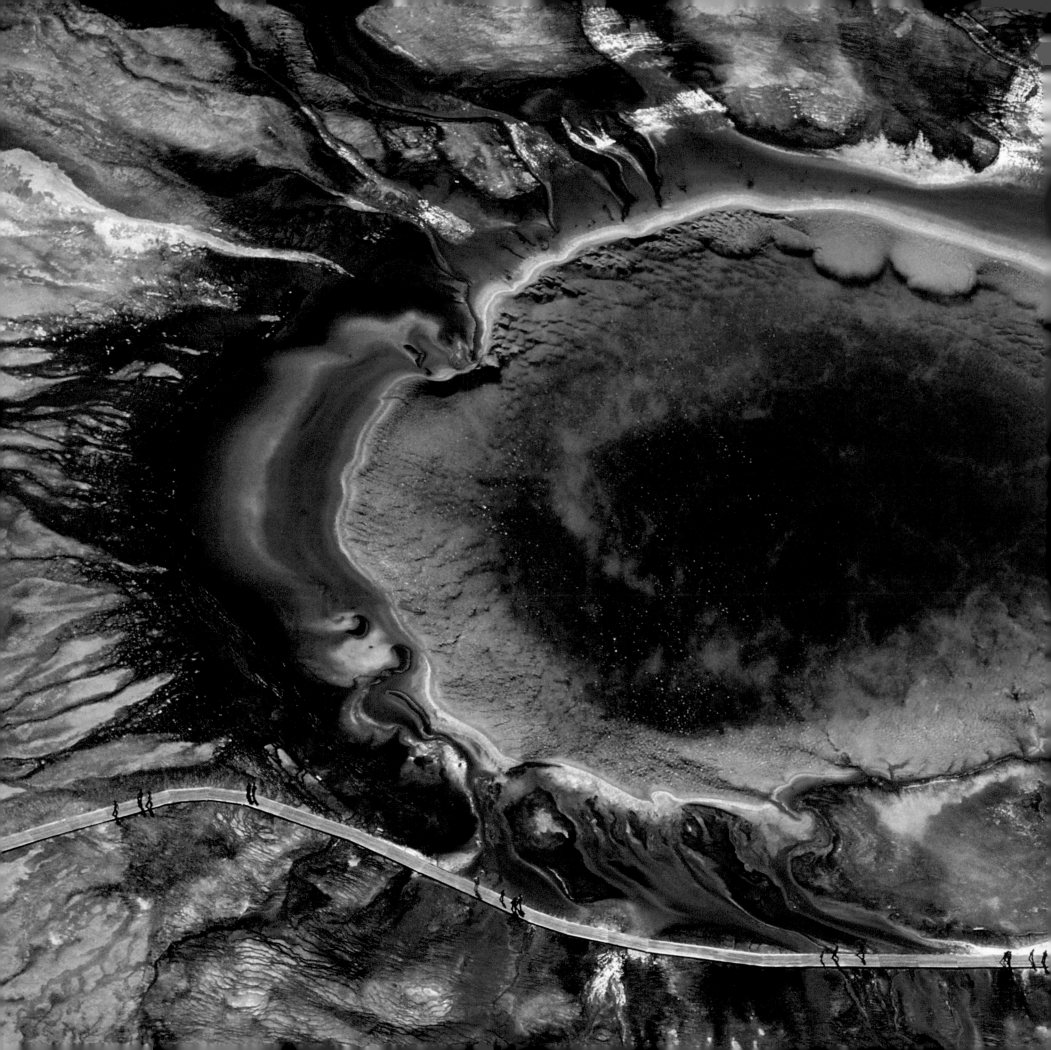

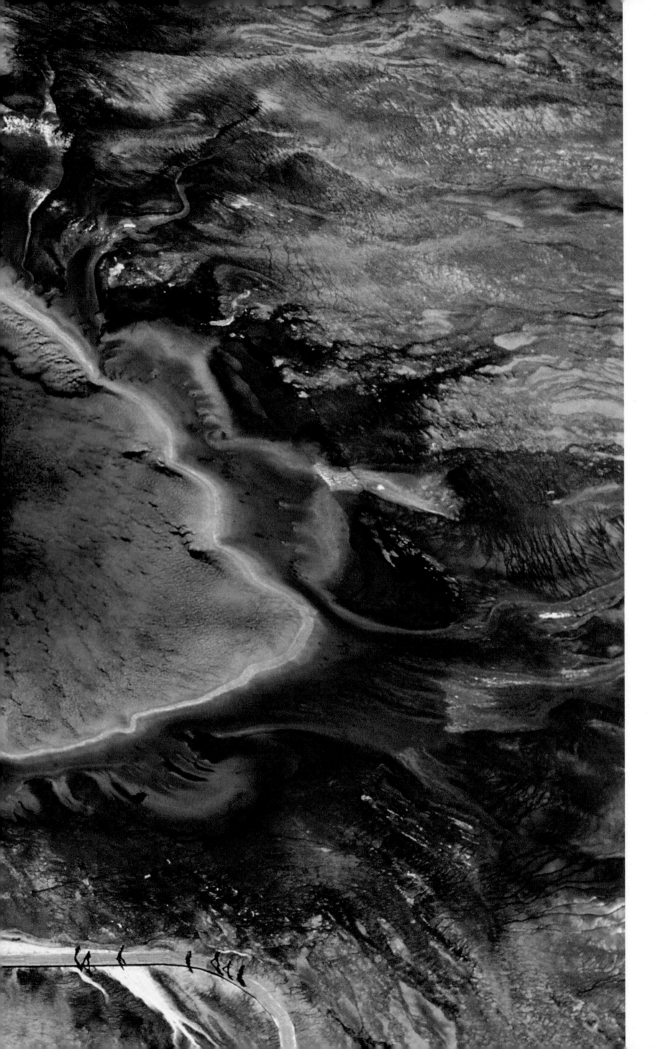

YELLOWSTONE NATIONAL PARK, Wyoming

Established in 1872, Yellowstone was the
first national park in the world. It preserves
more than 2 million acres of wilderness in
the northwest corner of Wyoming. Aside
from its remarkable array of geothermal
wonders—from geysers and fumaroles
(steam vents) to hot springs and mudpots—
Yellowstone comprises a vast plateau of
pine forests and meadows. The dramatic
coloring of the Prismatic Springs, pictured,
is caused by the algae and bacteria that
live in its mineral-rich waters.

HIGHWAY, Iowa (left)

Iowa, nicknamed the "Hawkeye State" after a fictional character who was a renowned outdoorsman, tamed most of its wilderness more than a century ago. Its gently rolling hills were once covered by prairie. Now corn and other crops grow abundantly in what is considered the heartland of American agriculture.

FARMLAND, Nebraska (right)

Nebraska was dismissed as a useless desert by some of its first European explorers. Subsequent waves of settlers re-evaluated its potential, and the "Cornhusker State" has since grown into one of the country's top farm producers, cultivating such crops as wild hay, sorghum, alfalfa, wheat and corn.

LAKE COEUR D'ALENE, Idaho
Light and fog filter through evergreens by
Lake Coeur d'Alene, one of Idaho's prettiest
lakes. Located in the state's 45-mile-wide
Northern Panhandle, the lake and nearby
tracts of wilderness have helped make Idaho
a favorite destination for campers, anglers,
hunters and those who value the attractions
of an unspoiled natural environment.

WILLIAMS COUNTY, North Dakota (above)

Having tumbled through the mountains of Montana, the Yellowstone and Missouri rivers converge near Williston, North Dakota. During the last ice age, the Missouri River marked the southern edge of America's glaciated regions. The pallid sturgeon, an endangered remnant of this time, has been bred in captivity in these rivers since 1998 in an attempt to save the species from extinction.

KANSAS CITY, Missouri (right)

Deserted now but not for long, the Arrowhead Stadium has hosted the Kansas City Chiefs football team since its completion in 1972. Featuring state-of-the-art design concepts, such as the world's first rolling stadium roof, the now-aging Arrowhead was a benchmark for stadium design. Although the Chiefs last won the Superbowl in 1970, scores of people still crowd the stadium each home game.

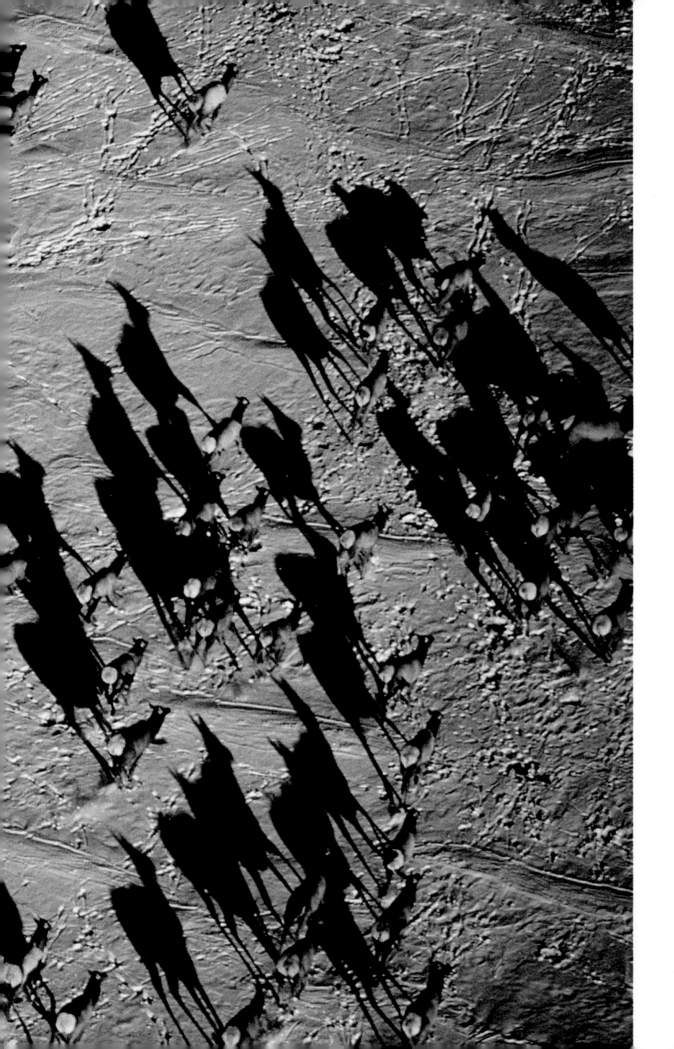

JACKSON HOLE, Wyoming

Golden in the afternoon sun, a herd of wapiti (*Cervus canadensis*) walk across the snow-covered landscape of Jackson Hole in Wyoming. Also known as the North American elk, this large member of the deer family was once prevalent throughout the continent. Years of hunting for food and sport, however, have significantly diminished its numbers. Most populations now exist under the protection of national parks and wildlife refuges.

ST. LOUIS, Missouri (left)

Brightly colored gravel barges offset the muddiness of the Mississippi River in the docklands of St. Louis. Named after King Louis IX of France, the city was originally a French fur-trading colony until, following the Louisiana Purchase of 1803, it became a part of the United States. Its position near the confluence of the Mississippi and Missouri rivers is still strategically important for trade.

KETCHUM, Idaho (right)

The mountains near Ketchum, Idaho, with their ski resorts and wilderness preserves, have been drawing large numbers of tourists since the Union Pacific Railroad came to the town in 1935. Originally a silver mining town until the bottom dropped out of silver prices in the 1890s, the once-sleepy town of Ketchum now relies on the tourist dollar for its livelihood.

BIG BADLANDS, South Dakota

South Dakota's Big Badlands are the world's best example of badlands topography, characterized by heavily eroded, steep rocky ridges, deep gullies and sparse vegetation. So-called because Native Americans and fur-trappers found the area difficult to cross, the Big Badlands is not only important geologically, but also contains the world's richest fossil beds from the Oligocene epoch, with fossils dating 35 to 25 million years old.

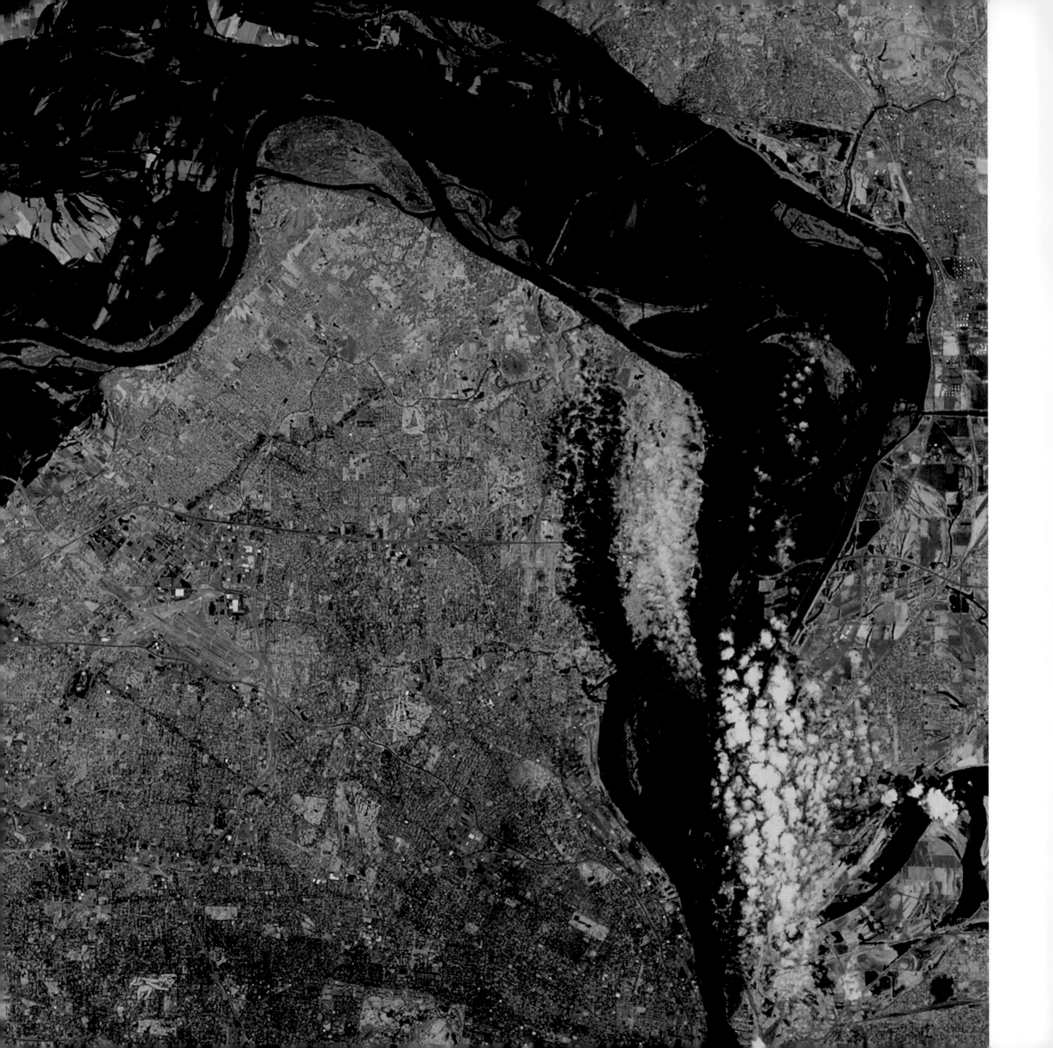

ST. LOUIS COUNTY, Missouri (left)

The blue-black waters of the Mississippi and Missouri rivers, seen here at the height of their flooding in 1993, form an almost impenetrable barrier in this Landsat satellite image. The city of St. Louis, colored purple at bottom center, is shielded from the inundation by floodwalls and levees.

WHEATFIELDS, Kansas (above)

Early explorers traveled to Kansas in search of gold. But it was the state's expansive golden wheatfields that would eventually sustain its population. The United States is the third largest producer of wheat in the world—a figure owed, in no small part, to Kansas' wheat industry.

MISSION RANGE, Montana

West of the Rocky Mountains in Montana
lies a popular tourist region centered
around Mission Valley, above which rise
the serrated ridges of the Mission
Mountains. Much of the land, including a
wilderness preserve famous for its bears,
belongs to the Flathead Indian Reservation.

WHEATFIELDS, North Dakota (above)

North Dakota's seemingly endless plains were found suitable for cultivating hardy species of wheat that can cope with the state's relatively short growing season. Agriculture is now the mainstay of the state's economy.

HIGH PLAINS, Nebraska (right)

The high plains of Nebraska were once roamed by herds of bison. The animals were hunted almost to extinction in the mid-nineteenth century, and their grazing fields—mixed grass steppes—were converted into agricultural land or ranching pastures.

GREAT PLAINS, Wyoming (left)

The Great Plains extend for 2,500 miles through the heart of the North American continent, including Wyoming. It is thought that the name Wyoming was originally derived from the Delaware Indian word *Maughwauwama*, meaning "large plains." While soils are generally sandy and poor, giving rise to landforms such as those pictured, the short-grass of the prairie is suitable for cattle and sheep ranching.

BLACK HILLS, South Dakota (right)

Trees accent the course of Black Hills Stream as it wends its way through western South Dakota. Known to the Lakota Indians as *Paha Sapa*, meaning "hills that are black," the region is studded with Ponderosa pines, which appear black when seen from a distance. Following the discovery of gold in 1874 by General Custer, prospectors and farmers rapidly settled in the region.

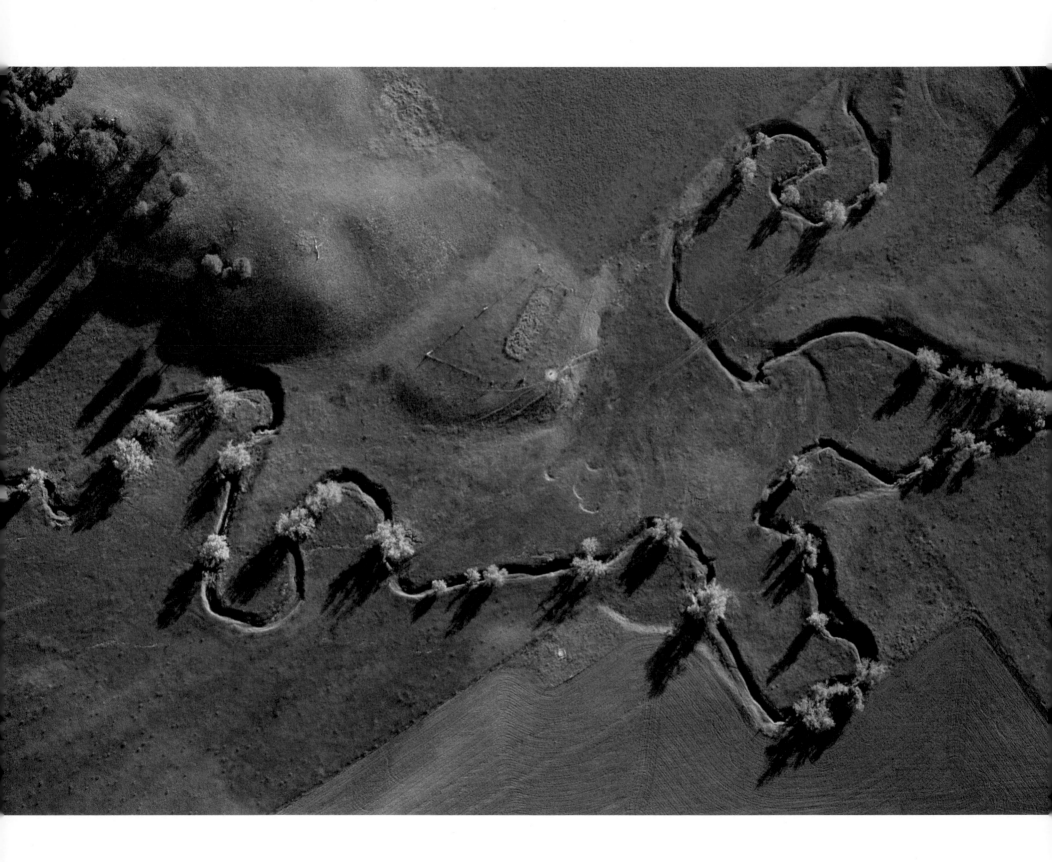

THE SOUTH WEST

ARIZONA ~ COLORADO ~ NEVADA
NEW MEXICO ~ TEXAS ~ UTAH

Though it belonged to Spain and Mexico for almost twice as long as it has been in American hands, the ruggedly beautiful South West in many ways symbolizes the United States of the world's popular imagination. Cowboys heading off Indians at a rocky pass; fortune-seekers searching for material and spiritual riches; adventurers setting off toward new horizons— the folklore, like its setting, is larger than life.

into Texas in the mid-1800s and soon declared the area an independent republic. The United States and Mexico (which had inherited the area from Spain) fought over the disputed territory, until Mexico surrendered and ceded the entire region from Texas to California to the victorious Americans. Like their independent-minded forebears, however, today's Texans think of their huge state as a place apart.

The steep canyons, sandy deserts and snow-capped mountains of the South West repelled many potential early settlers. Spain established only a few scattered regional outposts from the 1500s, but that was enough to antagonize Native American tribes and set an early precedent for the hostilities that would become the staple of Hollywood westerns. Lured by the wide open spaces, Americans trickled

Yet most of the South West remained sparsely populated even after the American government officially declared the national frontier "closed" in 1890. Rather than virtually give away the land to homesteaders, as it had in the Great Plains, the government maintained control over much of this region. Almost 90 percent of Nevada, for example, is public land.

SAM HOUSTON NATIONAL FOREST, Texas

Named for the victor of the battle at San Jacinto (and also Texas president, U.S. senator and state governor), Sam Houston National Forest in Texas sprawls across Montgomery, Walker and Dan Jacinto counties on the southern edge of the Piney Woods. Different areas within the park are set aside for camping, picnicking, hiking, fishing, swimming and boating.

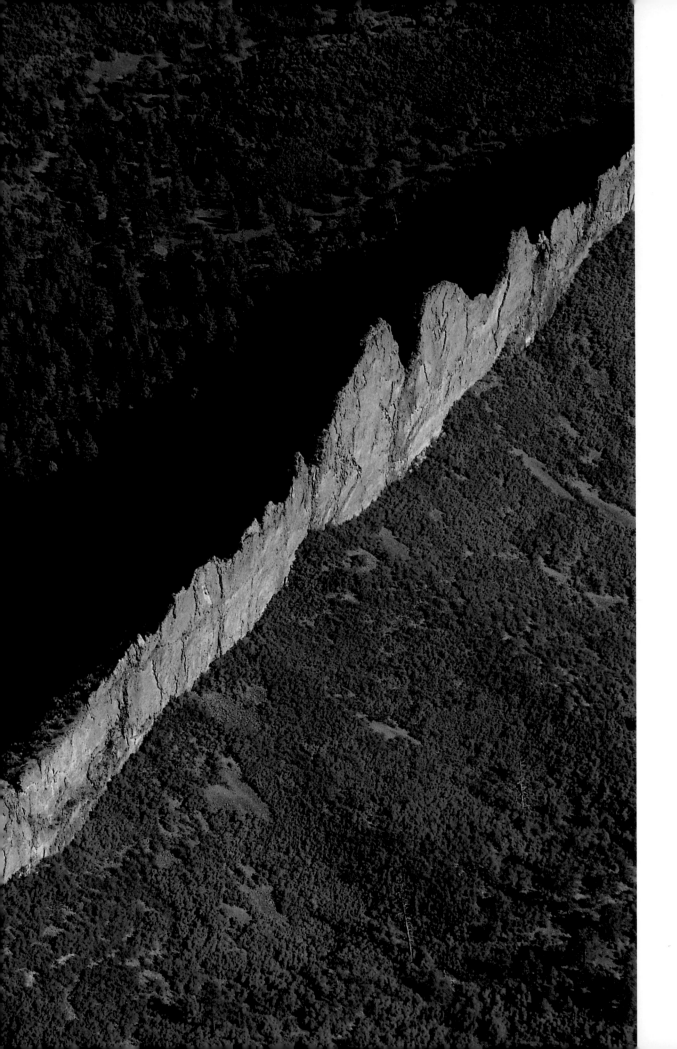

That does not guarantee public access, however, for this is where the military tests many of its weapons.

Energy and mining industries have enriched many pockets of the region, and cities such as Houston, Texas, and Denver, Colorado, flourished and sprawled as a result. Smaller mining towns that had emerged almost overnight faded nearly as quickly, and now remain as ghost towns for tourists.

The South West's scenic wonders, especially Arizona's stark Grand Canyon and Colorado's wildlife-rich Rocky Mountains, draw even more visitors, as do Colorado's ski resorts. Holding a different appeal is the entirely artificial playground of Las Vegas, Nevada, whose lavish casinos create intricate worlds on a scale that staggers the imagination. The region experienced dramatic population growth during the second half of the twentieth century. The influx has strained local water and land resources and driven home the stark reality that the South West's empty spaces, though still plentiful overall, are nevertheless finite.

SAN JUAN MOUNTAINS, New Mexico (left)

Northern New Mexico's mountainous terrain has become a magnet for mountain bikers and other adventure-sports lovers. The state boasts a remarkable geographic diversity, from Rocky Mountain ranges in the north to the Chihuahuan Desert in the south, the Great Plains to the east and spectacular canyons in the west.

DENVER, Colorado (above)

Denver International Airport opened in 1995 amid a storm of criticism and controversy. Massive cost overruns, delays and a faulty baggage handling system made it a laughing-stock, and its distance (24 miles) from the city made it unpopular. Since then residents have slowly come to accept it and even to admire its clean design.

TAOS GORGE BRIDGE, New Mexico

As it snakes through northern New Mexico, the Rio Grande flows through a crack in the Earth's surface—the Rio Grande Rift—and over time the river has cut deep gorges through the Taos Plateau. There is still some minor seismic activity along the rift, and a few hot springs testify to the proximity of subterranean hot rock. The Taos Gorge Bridge rises some 600 feet above the Rio Grande Gorge. This is the region's foremost whitewater rafting site.

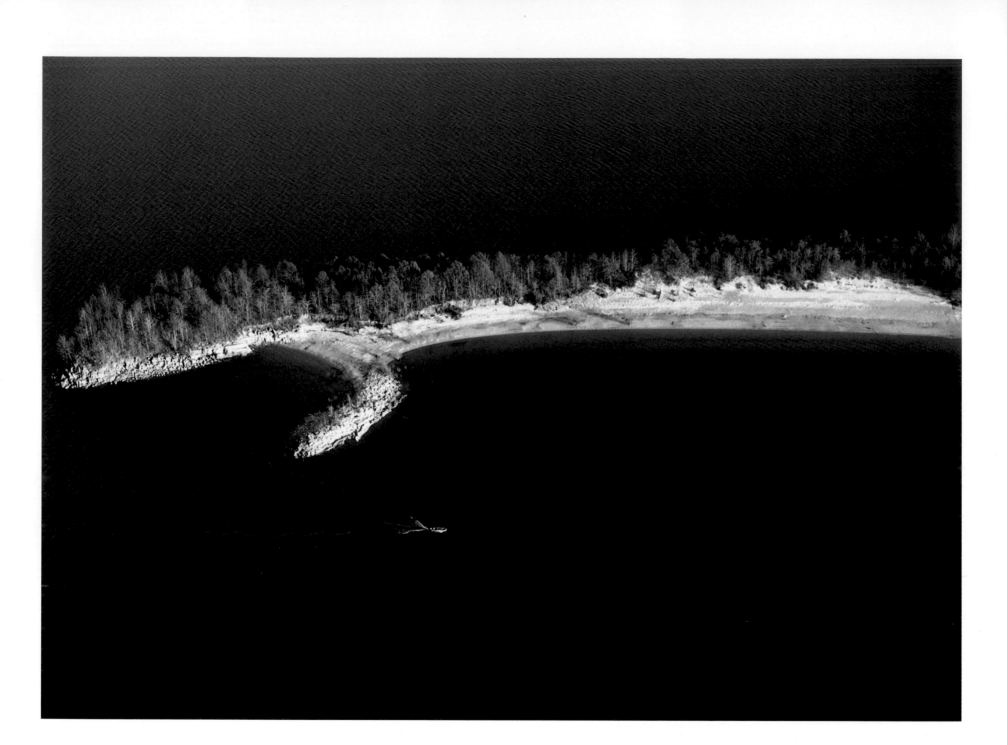

JASPER COUNTY, Texas (above)

An impounded river that winds through the woods, the Sam Rayburn reservoir covers 114,500 acres with a total capacity of 2,852,600 acre-feet. The two hydroelectric generating units at the dam have been producing energy since 1966. The facility is owned by the federal government and maintained by the U.S. Army Corps of Engineers.

SAN JUAN COUNTY, New Mexico (right)

Much of the land in the northwest corner of New Mexico belongs to the Navajo nation, who live in the country's largest Native American reservation. This distinctive landscape between Farmington and Shiprock, with its strange, twisting rock formations, has been formed by ancient volcanic upheavals then worn away by erosion.

MONUMENT VALLEY, Arizona

Monument Valley, lying on the border of
Arizona and Utah, is a high desert plateau
punctuated by dramatic mesas, buttes
and other rock formations. It has become
perhaps the region's most recognizable
scenic icon. The almost 30 thousand acres
of Monument Valley is located entirely
within the Navajo Indian reservation and
is self-administered by Navajo.

GRAND CANYON NATIONAL PARK,
Arizona (left)

The reds, oranges and greens of bigtooth
maples accent the natural russet features
of Point Imperial, overlooking Nankoweap
Canyon, in Grand Canyon National Park.
A World Heritage Site, the complex of
gorges carved by the Colorado River
system makes the Grand Canyon one of
the most spectacular examples of erosion
in the world.

**GREAT SAND DUNES NATIONAL
MONUMENT,** Colorado (right)

A thin band of snow defines light and
shade along the spine of a sand dune in
Great Sand Dunes National Monument,
near Alamosa in southern Colorado. With
the Sangre de Cristo Mountains as a jagged
backdrop, these sand dunes have been
carved by the wind into soft, twisted shapes
rising more than 700 feet into the air.

BRYCE CANYON NATIONAL PARK, Utah

Thousands of spires, protrusions, mazes and pinnacles make up the
unearthly horseshoe-shaped limestone, sandstone and mudstone
formations of Bryce Canyon National Park. Collectively known as
"hoodoos," these eerily delicate pillars and troughs are the complex
result of thousands of years of internal and external water erosion.
Water-soluble molecules dissolve inside the rock structures, and
water-borne debris scours away softer sedimentary layers.

LAS VEGAS, Nevada (left)

Located about 50 miles east of California and 30 miles west of Arizona, Las Vegas was originally a railroad town. In 1931 however, the construction of the Hoover Dam and the legalization of gambling triggered the city's current path of development. The urban sprawl pictured reflects Las Vegas' rapid growth.

PECOS RIVER, Texas (right)

One of the 540 species found in Texas, sandhill cranes inhabit the sandy hills along the Pecos River of the Llano Estacado. They are not an endangered species, unlike the whooping cranes for which they have been used as surrogate mothers.

LAKE POWELL, Arizona

Lake Powell, which straddles the
Arizona–Utah border, was formed by the
Colorado River's Glen Canyon Dam. Now
a National Recreation Area, the lake is a
magnet for watersports enthusiasts and
outdoor adventurers. The surrounding
region is rich in national parks and other
preserved areas.

RIO GRANDE VALLEY, Texas (left)

Although periodic freezes can devastate the region, the distinct semi-tropical climate of the lower Rio Grande Valley—the growing season can reach 341 days—has made it fruit and vegetable capital of the state. The valley is visited by thousands of northern "snowbirds," mostly from the Midwest, who seem to arrive and depart with the migrating geese.

WALKER LAKE, Nevada (right)

This false-color infrared image, taken from a Landsat satellite in 1987, shows the land use and topography of the area surrounding Walker Lake in Nevada. The black lozenge-shape feature at center is Walker Lake, while irrigated agricultural fields are seen here as a patchwork of pale green and yellow. The region's dependency on irrigation has caused the lake's water-level to drop approximately 130 feet in the last 120 years.

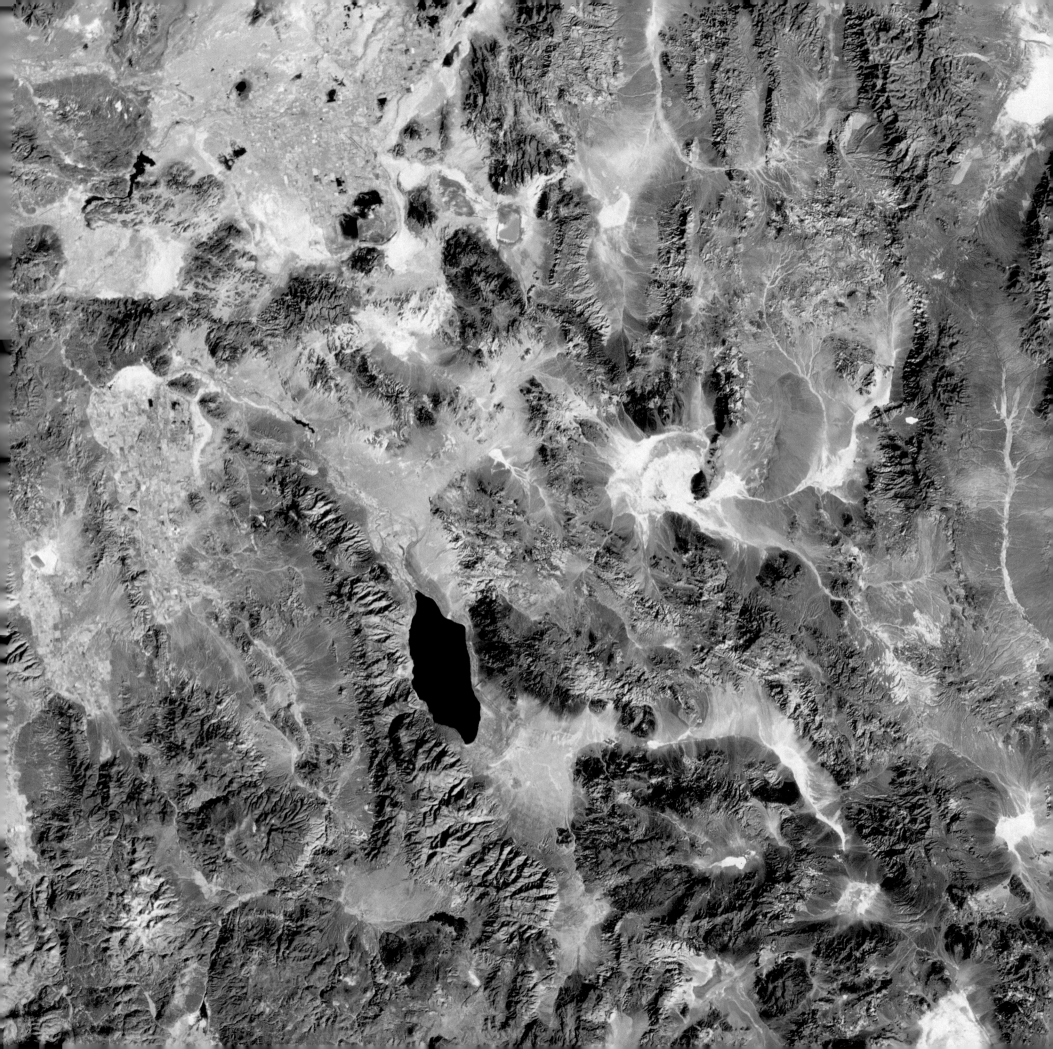

UNCOMPAHGRE NATIONAL FOREST, Colorado

Beneath the 14,150-foot peak of Mount Sneffels in the San Juan Mountains, a stand of quaking aspens changes color with the season. From the Ute word meaning "Where water makes red rock" the popular hunting grounds of the Uncompahgre Plateau stretch west across Colorado for approximately 70 miles, from the natural barrier of the Rockies.

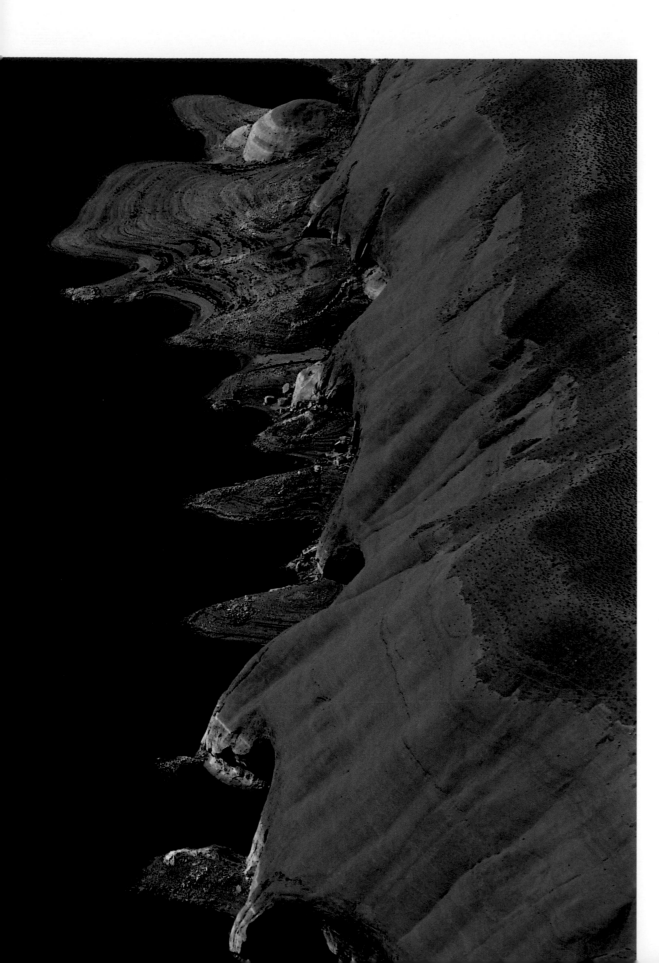

LAKE POWELL, Utah (left)

Because the Colorado River's natural flow is erratic, a series of dams were built to ensure that the lower portions of the river basin receive adequate water in drier years. One of these dams created Lake Powell, whose marinas in Arizona and Utah attract many vacationers.

ALBUQUERQUE, New Mexico (right)

From a small gathering of 13 balloonists in a parking lot in 1972, the Albuquerque International Balloon Fiesta has become the largest balloon event in the world and attracts thousands of visitors to the city in the first week of October each year. Such is the importance of the event that an International Balloon Museum is currently under construction.

BLACK CANYON, Nevada

At more than 6 million tons in weight and 760 feet in height, Hoover Dam is one of the largest concrete dams ever built. Thousands of men built the dam and power plant complex, working from April 1931, when site preparation began, until May 1935, when the last concrete was poured. The dam was designed principally to provide low-cost electricity for southwest America, and blocks the 1,400-mile-long Colorado River as it makes its way from the mountains of Colorado to the Gulf of California.

COLORADO NATIONAL MONUMENT, Colorado (left)

Two climbers take a welcome rest on the summit on Monument Spire in Colorado National Monument, near Grand Junction. Created in 1911, the Monument is a series of sandstone formations including canyons, pinnacles and monoliths. It is home to numerous species of plants and wildlife.

PADRE ISLAND NATIONAL SEASHORE, Texas (right)

Only now receiving worldwide recognition, the pristine beach at Padre Island is located at the southernmost tip of the Texas Gulf Coast. Home to Kemp's ridley sea turtle—the world's most endangered—Padre is the longest undeveloped barrier island in the world. Most of the island can be explored only on foot.

AZTEC RUINS NATIONAL MONUMENT,
New Mexico

Erroneously named by early explorers, the "Aztec" Ruins of New Mexico are in fact Anasazi Indian ruins dating from about 1100 to 1200 AD. Used by tribes associated with both the Pueblo Indians of Chaco Canyon, to the south, and Mesa Verde, to the north, the site is a complex of small residential houses, large multi-story "great houses," kivas and segments of road.

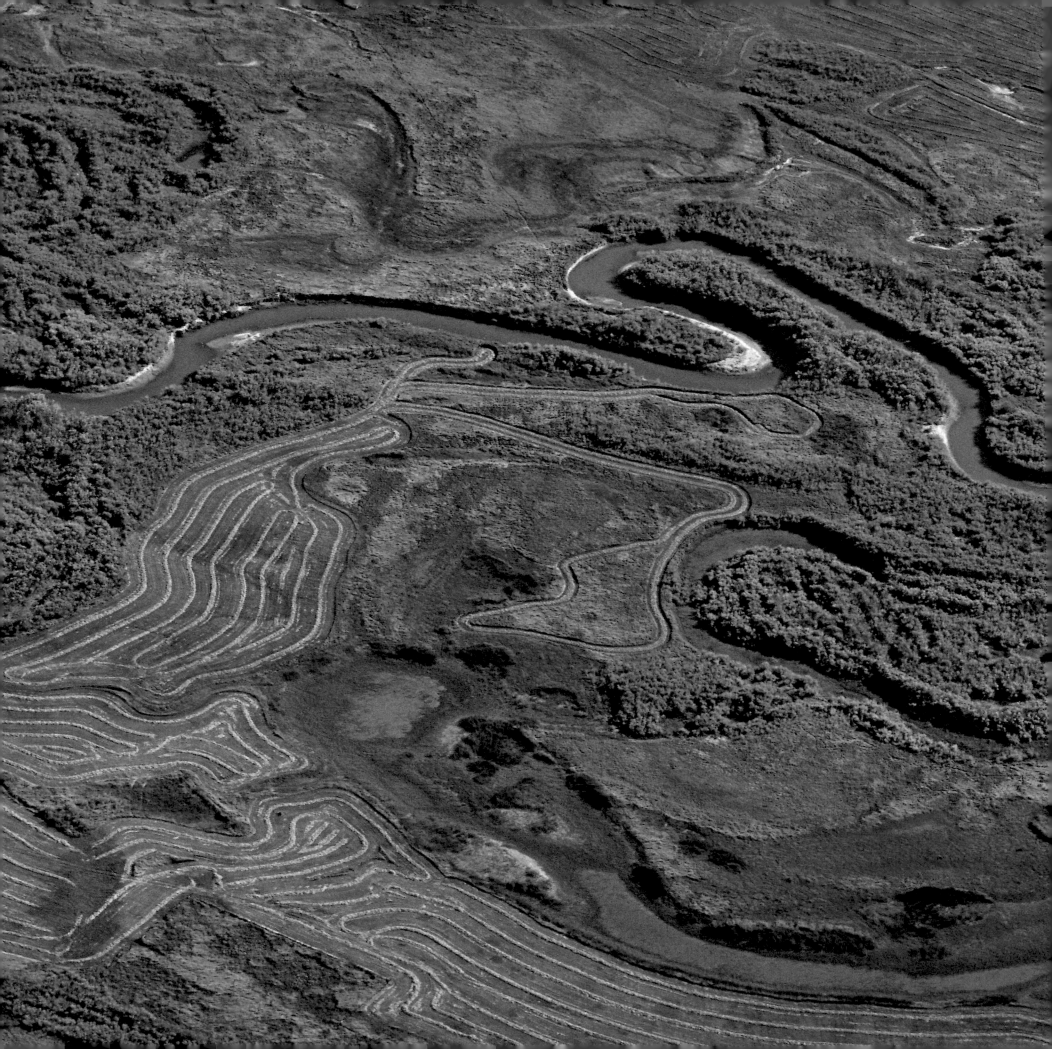

HIGH DESERT, Nevada (left)

Nevada is the driest state in the nation.
Rivers that have not been diverted for
irrigation typically disappear in alkaline
sinks. But this arid land is rich in minerals,
and mining towns have risen and fallen as
deposits have been discovered and exploited.
Rain in central Nevada is infrequent but can
be tumultuous, resulting in flash floods.

PAINTED DESERT, Arizona (right)

Northeast Arizona's badlands are known as
the Painted Desert, thanks to the irregularly
eroded sedimentary and clay layers visible in
the rock formations. The red hues that typify
the area result from iron oxides in the soil.
Crusty patches of alkaline material combine
with the red surface to create a scaly,
multicolored palette. The Painted Desert is
part of Arizona's Petrified Forest National Park.

POTASH MINE, Utah

Utah is rich in mineral wealth. One of the
many minerals it produces is a potassium
compound known as potash, used in the
manufacture of soft soaps, among other
things. In his 1920 traveler's guide, F.D.B.
Gay described the "vast deposits, beds and
lodes" of alumite ore being refined at a mill
outside Marysvale as "sufficient to supply
the United States with pure potash and
potash-fertilizer during centuries to come."

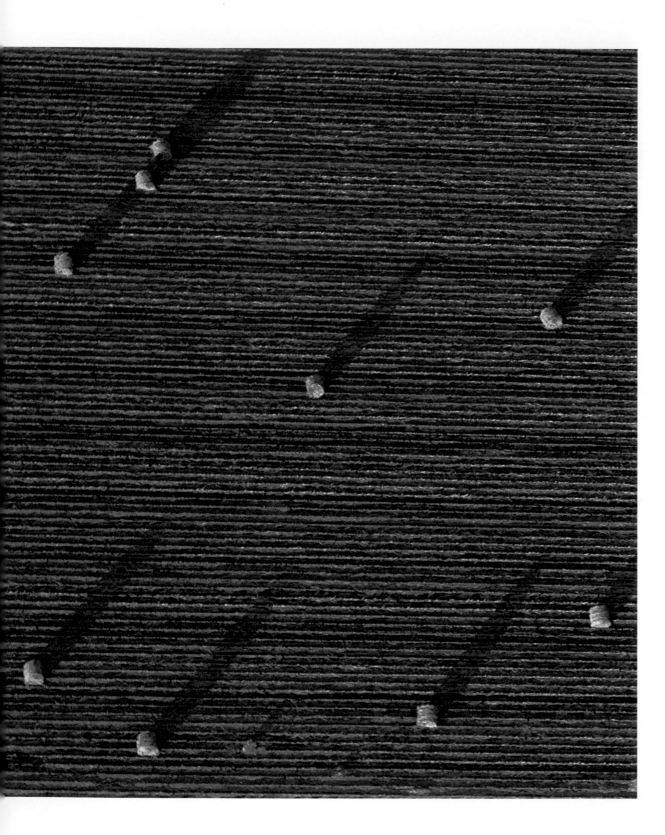

HALE COUNTY, Texas (left)

Hay is an important crop in cattle country, and in Hale County it is produced both for local use and for sale in other parts of Texas, especially during drought or periods when range cattle must be fed. The hay is cut and baled by machine, then fork-lifted onto trucks for transportation.

MAROON BELLS–SNOWMASS WILDERNESS AREA, Colorado (right)

Colorado's Maroon Bells–Snowmass Wilderness Area is interlaced with hiking trails. Its defining features are two peaks—known as the Maroon Bells—rising more than 14,000 feet above Maroon Lake.

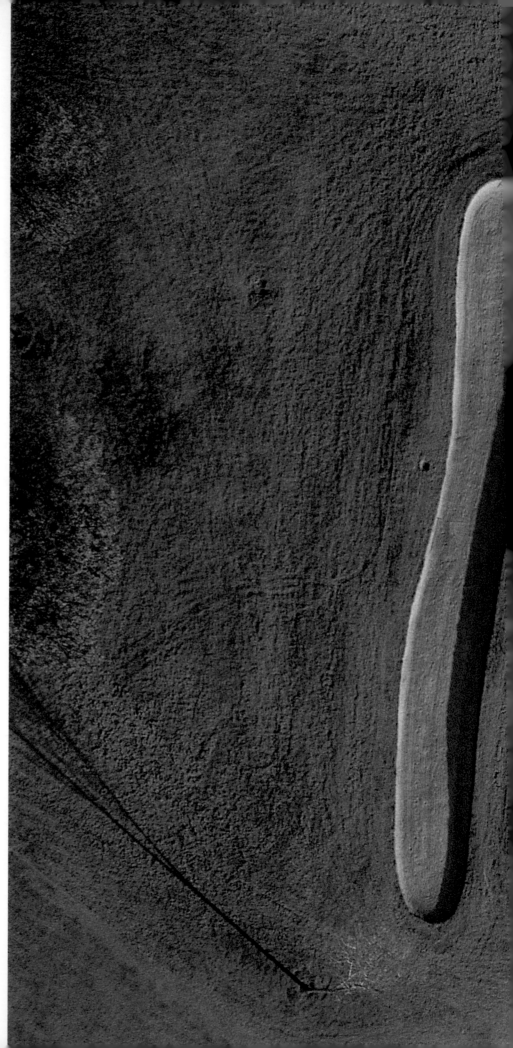

ABILENE, Texas

Prosperity has brought all the appurtenances of modern civilization
to West Texas, and this includes the game invented by the Scots
some centuries back. Fairways and greens require continual watering
in this climate, and water hazards are almost always artificial—but
there is no shortage of the materials to make sand traps to challenge
players at Fairway Oaks Golf Course.

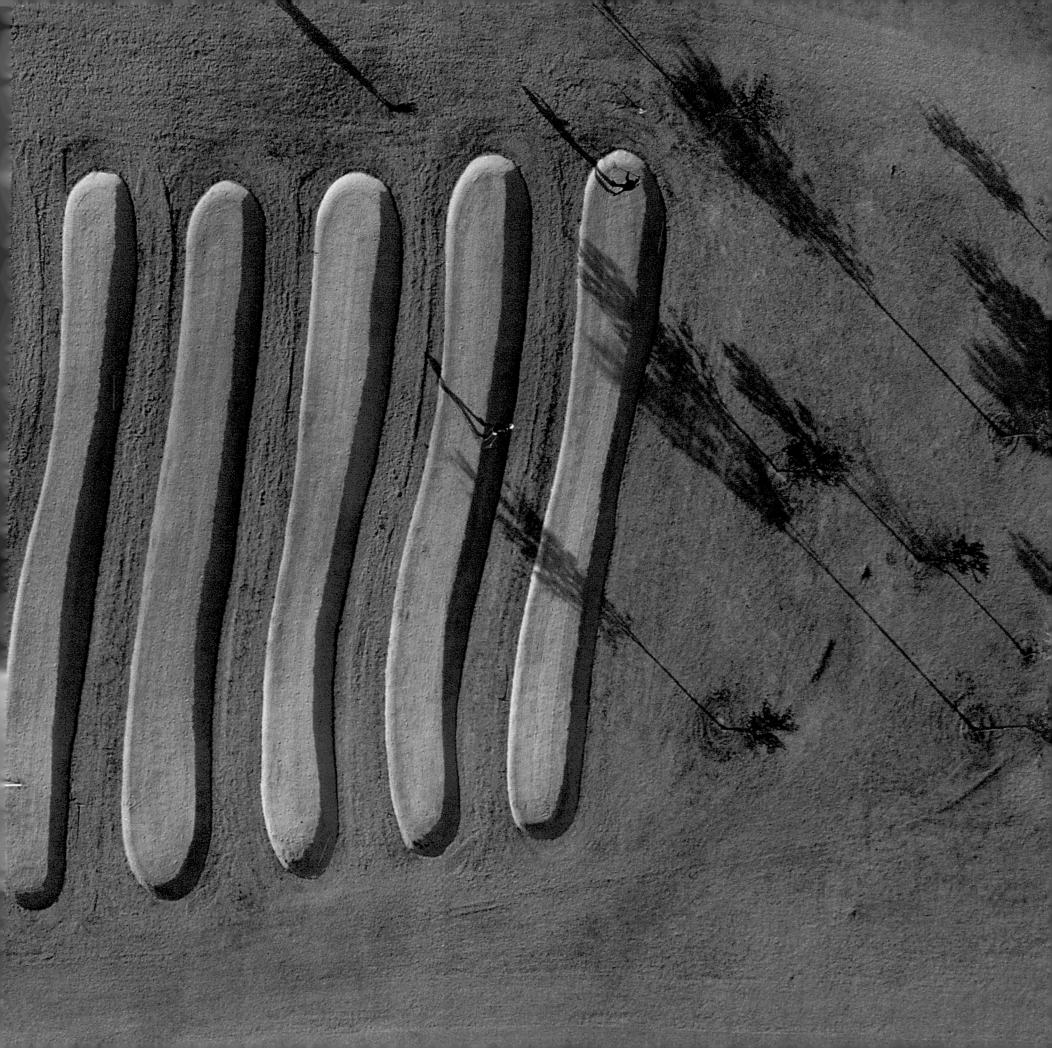

LAS VEGAS, Nevada (left)

Las Vegas' "Strip" is lined by casinos whose spectacularly lit exteriors turn night into day. Their stage shows and gambling tables attract visitors from around the world. Spanish for "the meadows," Las Vegas was named by traders impressed by the valley's abundant native grasses and plentiful water. The city was incorporated in 1911; 20 years later, gambling was legalized and its future was assured.

MONUMENT VALLEY, Arizona (right)

The dramatic Monument Valley, on the Utah–Arizona border, is the most enduring image of the American West, and was the setting for many classic westerns. Imposing red mesas and butte formations rise up to 1,000 feet from the vast, seemingly barren land. The crumbling formations are the last remnants of the sandstone layers that once covered the region.

THE PACIFIC STATES

ALASKA ❧ CALIFORNIA ❧ OREGON ❧ WASHINGTON

America's west coast is a study in contrasts. It stretches from southern California's warm, sunny beaches to Alaska's glacier-carved wilderness, with the often-rainy, richly forested states of Oregon and Washington in between.

Canada's British Columbia province separates Alaska from the contiguous mainland states; in fact, Alaska is much closer to Russia than to its nearest American neighbors. This isolation has helped the nation's largest, but second-least-populated, state retain a certain frontier atmosphere. Another factor that sets it apart is its racial composition: Inuit and Native Americans were Alaska's primary inhabitants until the beginning of the twentieth century, and the state still has a significant indigenous population. When the American government purchased the territory from Russia in 1867 for about 7 million dollars, the transaction was derided as "Seward's Folly," in honor of the man who sealed the deal. But this proved to be one of the shrewdest real estate transactions in history, for, far from being a frozen wasteland, Alaska turned out to be rich in oil and other natural resources. Government and the mining industry now employ a large proportion of its mostly male workforce.

California, by contrast, is America's most populous state. Only a few Spanish missions and forts shared the large territory with its indigenous inhabitants until an 1849 gold rush lured tens of thousands of fortune-seekers to the area, shortly after it was ceded to the United States. Since then, California's mild climate and tolerant views have steadily attracted domestic and overseas migrants searching for their slice of paradise, even if it lies astride an active earthquake fault line.

WALLA WALLA COUNTY, Washington

Each year in May, thousands of spectators come to Walla Walla County to the high school campus, or the county fairgrounds, to watch the ascent of dozens of balloons at the annual Hot Air Balloon Stampede. Begun in 1975, the Stampede is the first and most prestigious hot air balloon rally in the Pacific Northwest, and attracts some of the country's finest pilots.

Growth-related problems have in recent years convinced many Californians to head to the less-crowded, clean-living states of Oregon and Washington. But the romance of California continues to exert a strong pull, fueled in part by the Hollywood myth-making machine. California is more racially diverse than its northern neighbors, but its Spanish-speaking population is by far its most prominent subgroup. This has less to do with the area's colonial legacy—reflected in its suburban architecture and Spanish place names—and more to do with Latin American economic migrants in search of seasonal work.

Its proximity to the Mexican border has helped Los Angeles grow into the country's second-largest metropolis. The region's other large port cities, such as San Francisco, California, and Seattle, Washington, have forged strong commercial links with the other countries of the Pacific Rim. Their most valuable economic asset, however, has been high-technology industry that has reached a critical mass in such centers as Silicon Valley, south of San Francisco.

MOUNT HOOD NATIONAL FOREST, Oregon (left)

Some 20 miles east of Portland, this National Forest contains more than 189,000 acres of wilderness, including the volcanic Mount Hood's peak—the highest in Oregon—and upper slopes. The forested mountains, pristine lakes and icy streams attract outdoor sports lovers, such as hikers, mountaineers and cross-country skiers.

SAN FRANCISCO, California (above)

At more than eight miles, the double-decked San Francisco–Oakland Bay Bridge is one of the longest steel bridges in the world. Connecting San Francisco with the East Bay cities of Oakland and Berkeley, and the Bay Area's many suburbs, the Bay Bridge carries the bulk of local commuter traffic, an average of 280,000 vehicles a day.

KNOTT'S BERRY FARM, California (above)

In 1920 Walter and Cordelia Knott leased a 20-acre block of land near Buena Park in Orange County. Following the success in the 1930s of the first crops of boysenberries and Mrs. Knott's famous 65-cent chicken dinners, America's first theme park was created, built adjacent to the restaurant to entertain waiting lines of diners. Today, Knott's Berry Farm features shows, exhibits and rides, including these "Tubs of Fun."

SEATTLE, Washington (right)

Seattle is encompassed by water: the sound to the west, Lake Washington to the east, and a scattering of lakes, ponds and fountains throughout the city. The most desirable properties are those on the waterfront with a mountain view. Coming replete with personal jetties, they give substance to the locals' claim that Seattle has more boats per capita than any other American city.

LOS ANGELES, California (left)

When Liberace ordered a swimming pool, he wanted it in the shape of a piano. That made perfect sense. Los Angeles—a city that long since featured hot dog stands in the shape of dachshund pups, orange juice stands in the shape of oranges, and restaurants shaped like giant brown derbies—could easily assimilate a piano-shaped swimming pool.

MOUNT BAKER-SNOQUALMIE NATIONAL FOREST, Washington (right)

Located just south of the former mining town of Monte Cristo, a glacial lake in the North Cascade Mountain Range gleams with the reflected light of the summer sun. This u-shaped valley is part of the Mount Baker-Snoqualmie National Forest, a complex of wilderness areas stretching for more than 140 miles in northwestern Washington.

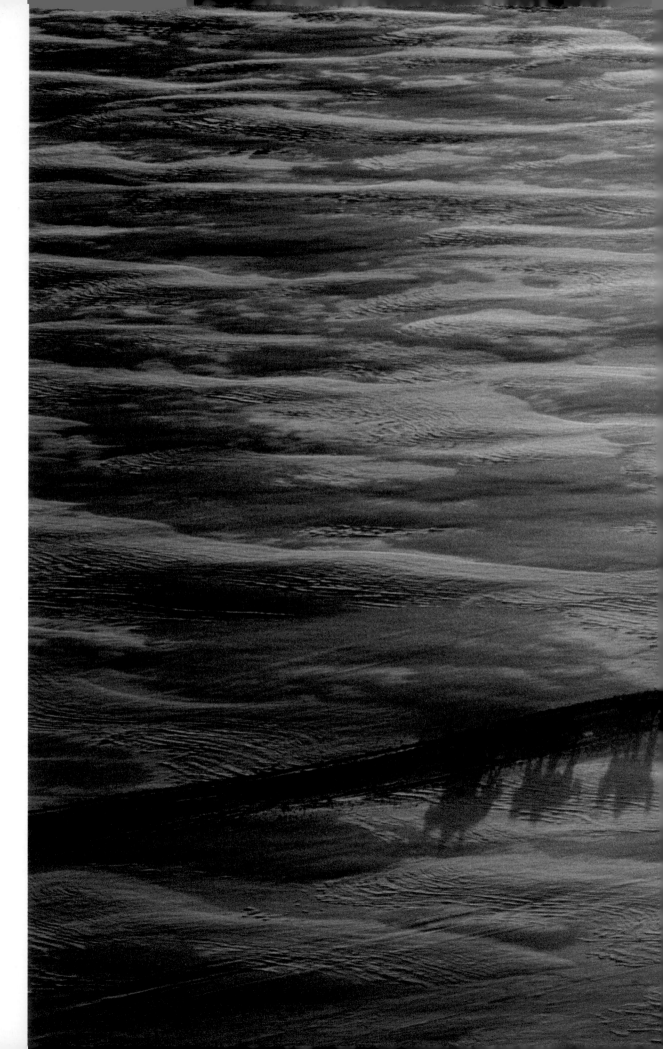

NORTON SOUND, Alaska

The Iditarod Trail Sled Dog Race brings
competitors from around the world to
Alaska every March. The mushers and their
dogs travel from Anchorage, Alaska, to
Nome, on the Bering Strait, more than 1,000
miles away across challenging mountain
and valley terrain. There are two routes,
northern and southern, which are used on
alternating years. The winning teams can
complete the trip in about nine days.

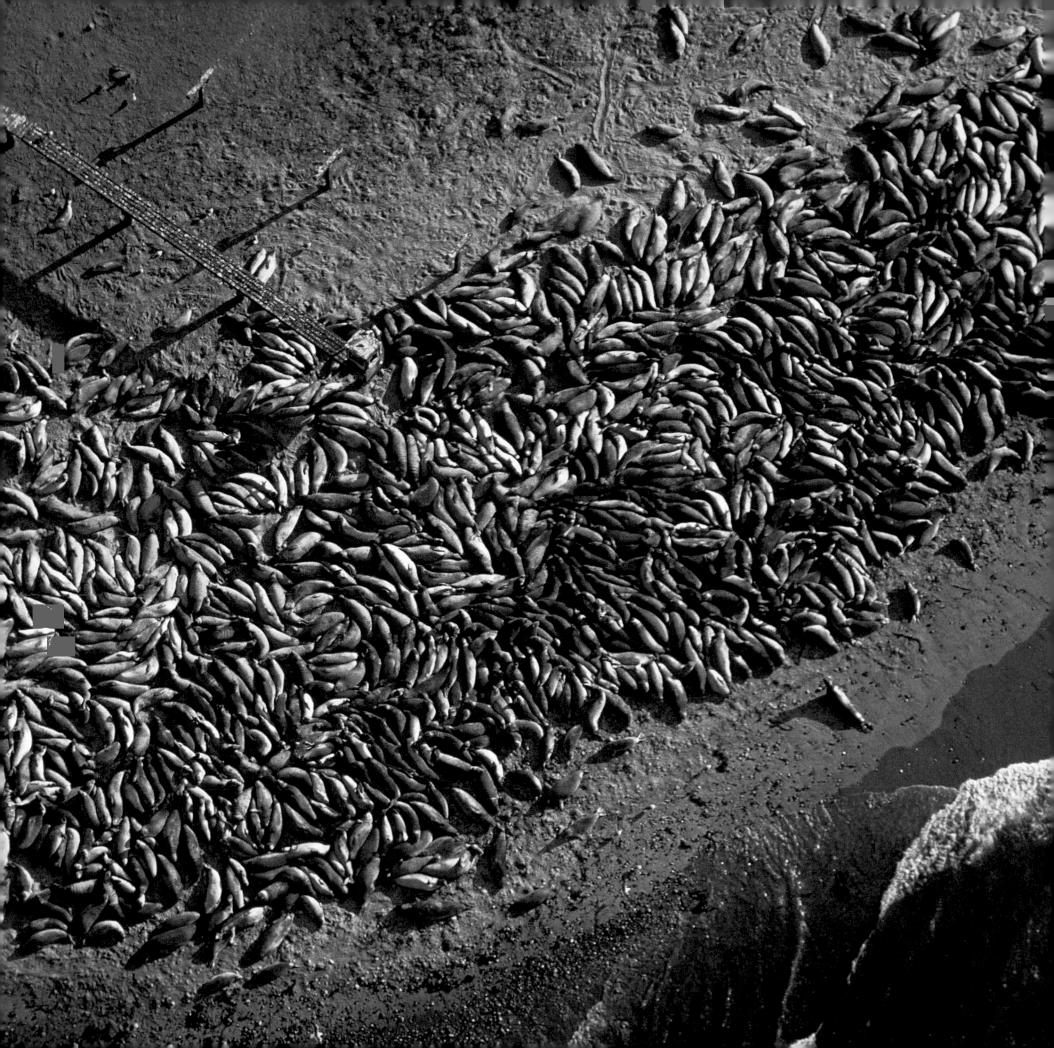

AÑO NUEVO STATE RESERVE, California (left)

Located north of Santa Cruz, Año Nuevo is a refuge for thousands of young Californian sea lions. Hunted to near extinction in the nineteenth century, the sea lions, along with other native marine mammals, have made a remarkable comeback under protection. Closed to the public, Año Nuevo Island is an important site for research into sea lion and seal breeding habits.

FEDERAL WAY, Washington (right)

Sunbathers drying off, or simply displaying themselves, create a mosaic at the Wild Waves Water Park. Named from a school that, in turn, was named for Highway 99 running parallel to Interstate 5 between Tacoma and Seattle, Federal Way is one of the nation's fastest growing communities.

CRATER LAKE NATIONAL PARK,
Oregon

Seven thousand years ago, Mount Mazama, Oregon, exploded in an eruption of magma and pyroclastic ash, before collapsing into a jagged caldera. Isolated from surrounding streams and rivers, Crater Lake slowly evolved as rain and melted snow filled the caldera. Today, at almost 2,000 feet, Crater Lake is the deepest in the United States and its vivid blue waters are some of the clearest in the world.

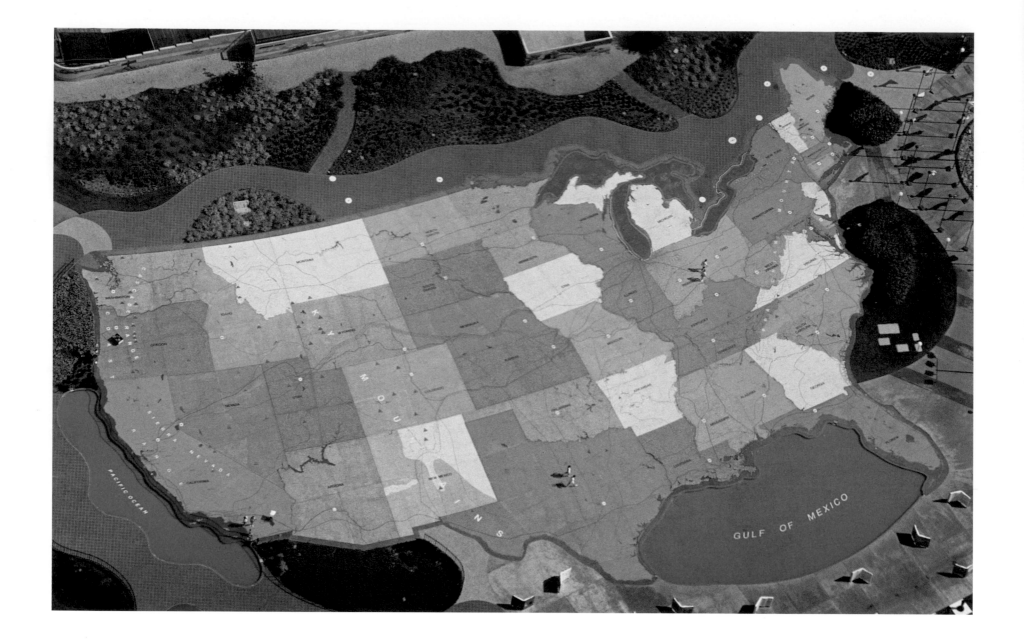

SAN DIEGO, California (above)

On yet another sunny day, visitors to the Sea World theme park in Mission Bay, San Diego, stroll across a pavement map of the United States. In the mid-nineteenth century it took six months to make the overland journey to California. The completion of the transcontinental railroad in 1869 reduced the journey to just over a week.

HANFORD, Washington (right)

A circle sprinkler fed by water from the federal irrigation system paints an abstract in alfalfa on the once arid plain near the Hanford Nuclear Reservation. In the years following the Civil War, a network of dams and irrigation works was constructed, providing water for imported crops and stimulating large-scale settlement of the area.

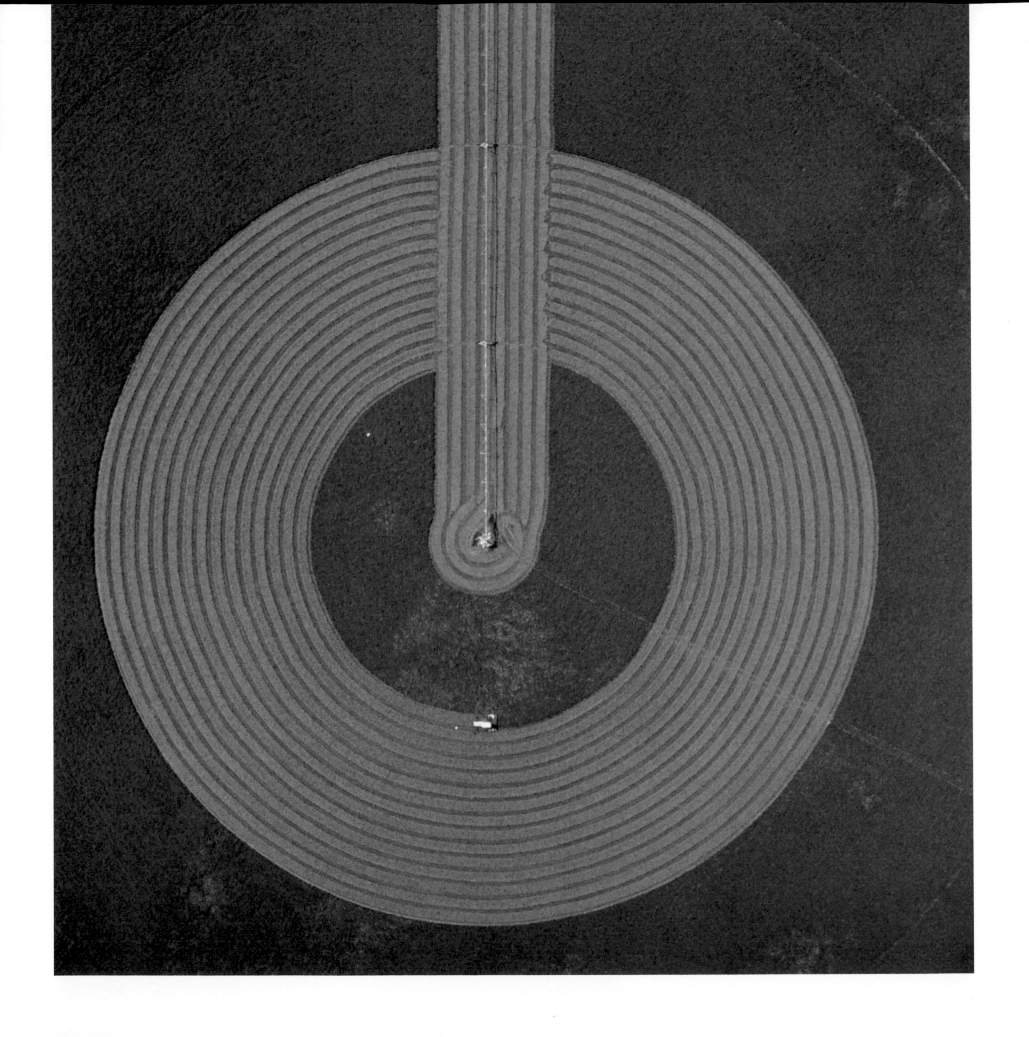

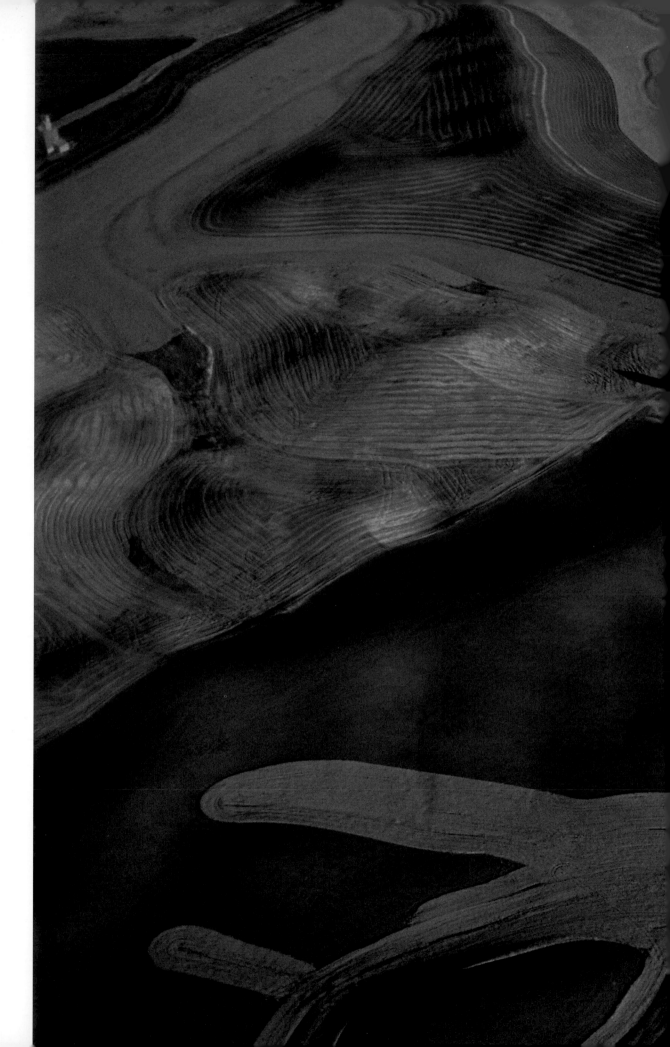

PALOUSE HILLS, Washington

Strip farming is much practiced in the
Palouse wheatfields of eastern Washington.
Bands of fallow soil lie between the
contoured strips of ripening grain. Light in
color and light in weight, the Palouse loess
is carried in by wind and water. It darkens
at the surface as organic matter decays.

TEHACHAPI PASS, California (left)

California poppies (*Eschscholztia californica*) tint an arid hillside with a wash of saffron. As the official state flower, California poppies are protected in this nature reserve near Tehachapi Pass. They are still the most common flower in the countryside and are often found growing in the cracks of city sidewalks.

SANDY POINT, Washington (right)

Located within the Lummi Indian Reservation, the leased land of Sandy Point separates the shallow waters of Bellingham Bay from Hale Passage. The Lummi were granted federal recognition in 1855, and today own 7,000 acres of coastal land on Puget Sound, earning their living mainly through fishing and shellfish operations.

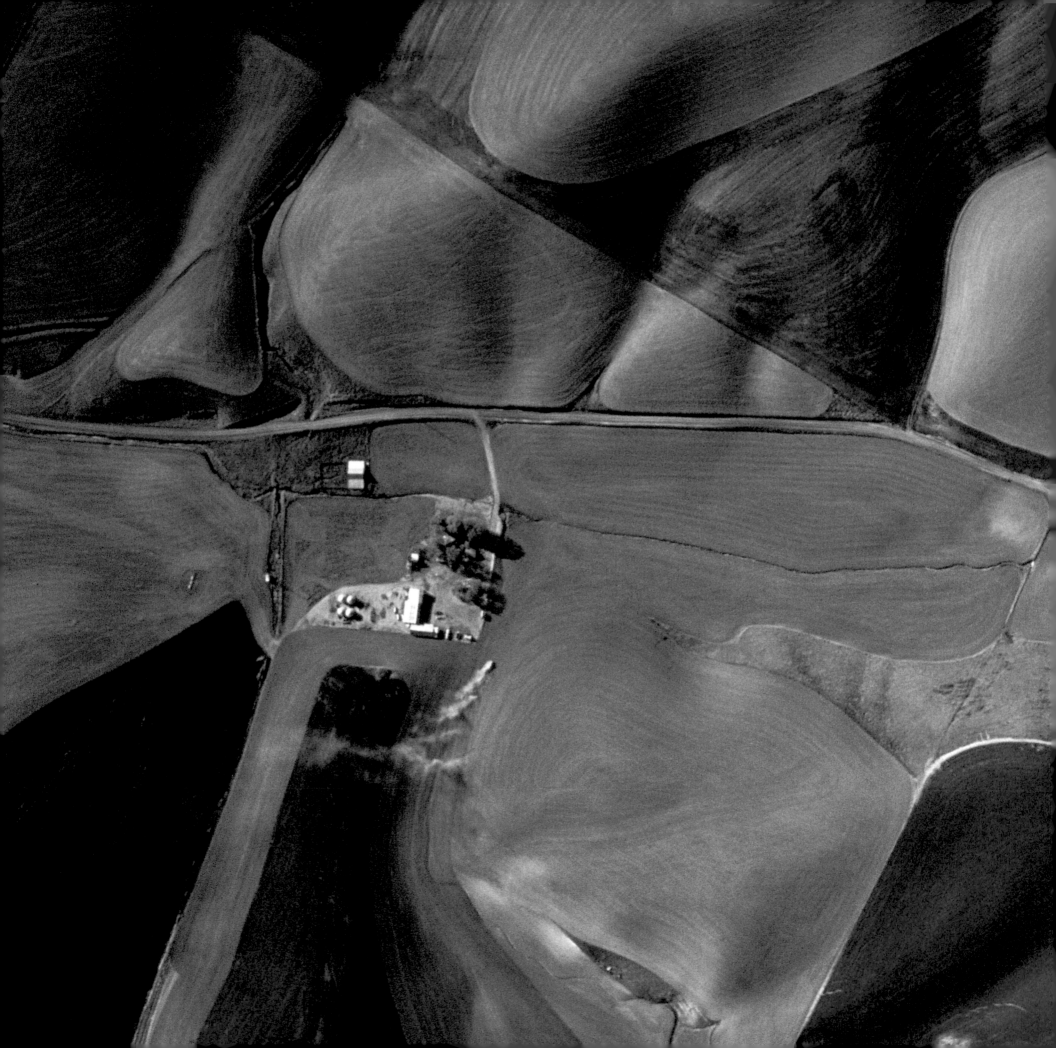

WALLA WALLA COUNTY,
Washington

Ever since sod was broken to raise food
for gold prospectors, wheat has been the
dominant crop on the rolling hills of Walla
Walla County, eastern Washington. The
topographical isolation of the region,
caused by the Cascade Range, was
overcome through the entrepreneurial
efforts of banker Dorsey Baker in 1867.
Baker became a folk legend by building
the "Rawhide Railroad"—so called for the
leather thongs that tied strips of strap iron
to the wooden rails—to carry grain from
the hinterland to the Columbia River and
downstream to Portland.

SAN FRANCISCO, California (left)

Forming a golden arc across San Francisco
Bay at sunset, the Bay Bridge is out-shone
only by the Oakland Docks, at left. The
berths of these docklands have been the
hub of the region's maritime industry
since the 1962 construction of the first
container port on the West Coast. The use
of containers dramatically increased the
cargo tonnage able to be carried by ships
and rejuvenated the industry.

SAN ANDREAS FAULT,
California (right)

The San Andreas fault is shown here running
across the bottom of the image, intersected
by the Garlock fault. Caused by the collision
of the Pacific and North American plates,
the San Andreas extends through California
for more than 600 miles. In the Great San
Francisco earthquake of 1906, which
measured 8.3 on the Richter Scale, the
Pacific Plate jumped 20 feet to the north.

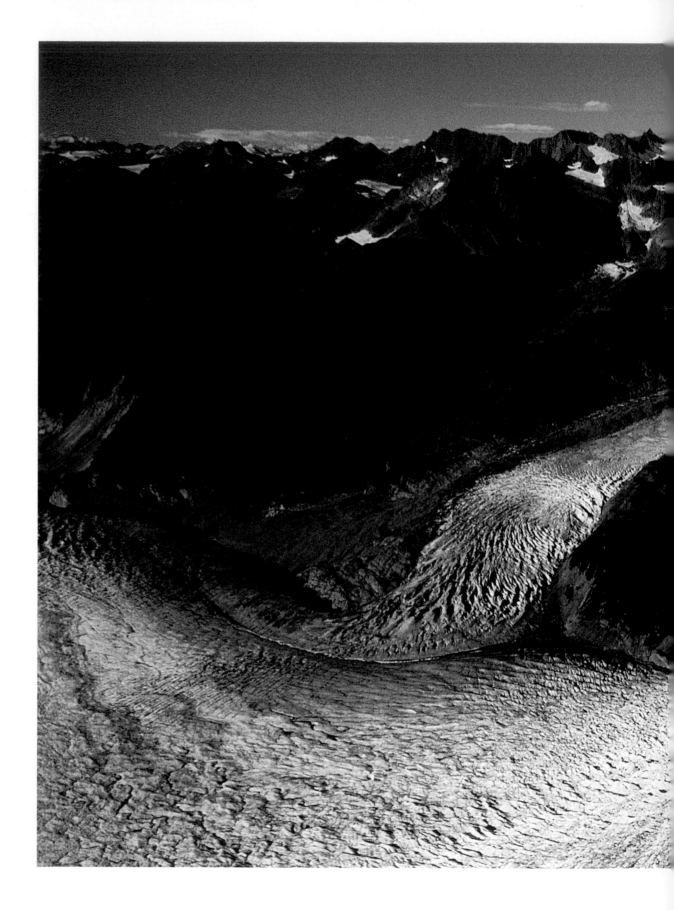

MOUNT McKINLEY, Alaska

Glaciers extend down the slopes of Alaska's
20,320-foot-high Mount McKinley, also
known by its Native American name, *Denali*,
which means "The High One." To the
disappointment of many tourists, North
America's highest peak is enshrouded by
clouds two out of every three days in
summer. The dark stripes in the center of
each glacier are trapped soil and debris that
will eventually be released to form large
piles of material known as moraines.

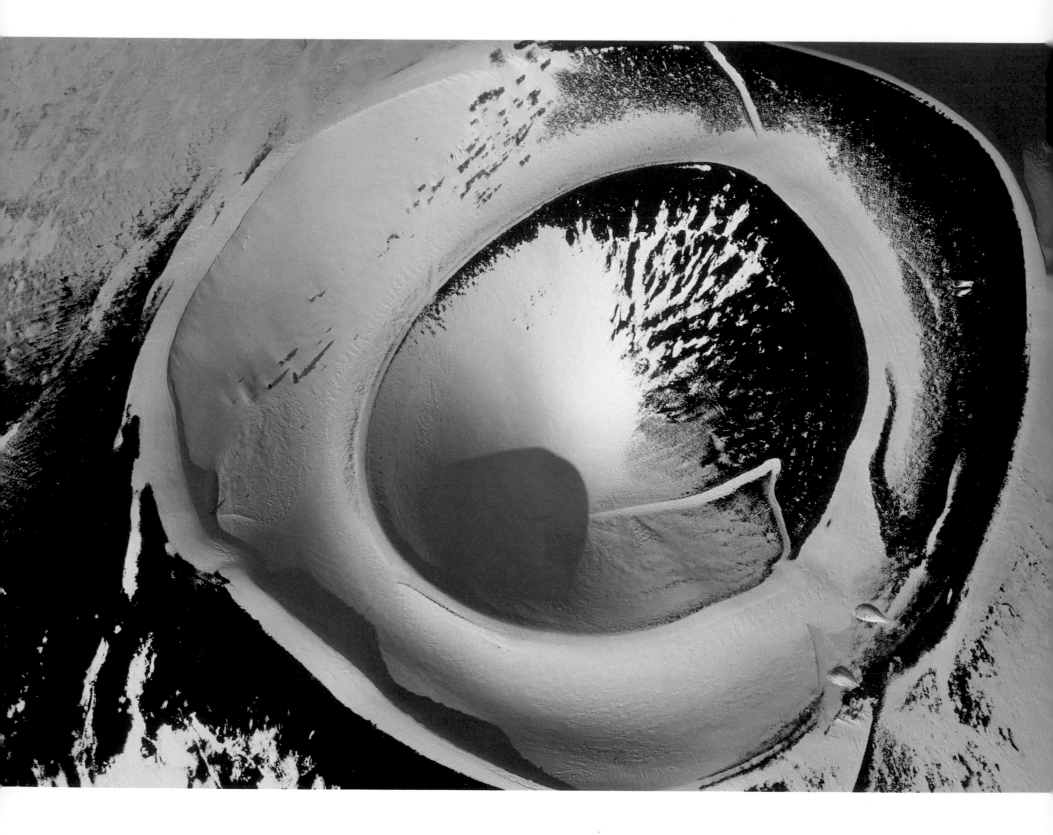

LASSEN VOLCANIC NATIONAL PARK, California (left)

Active for 200,000 years, Mount Tehama in Lassen Volcanic National Park, near Mineral in northeastern California, now lies dormant. Cracks and vents in the main cone caused magma to be drawn away into subsidiary volcanoes on its flanks, such as Mount Lassen, and Mount Tehama to crumble. This cinder cone is all that remains—a dramatic suggestion of the fiery convulsions that still shape the Modoc Plateau.

SILVANA, Washington (right)

Many Scandinavian immigrants were attracted to the lumber and farming area on the delta of the Stillaguamish River in western Washington. In the late nineteenth century they created this severe but beautiful Lutheran church at Silvana, near the town of Arlington.

POINT REYES NATIONAL SEASHORE, California

As mists slowly swirl and rise above the sea, the golden cliffs of the Point Reyes National Seashore greet the morning. Established by President Kennedy in 1962, the Seashore is a protected oasis of natural flora and fauna located just north of San Francisco. One-fifth of California's flowering plant species can be found here, along with 23 threatened and endangered species. With more than 360 recorded species, Point Reyes is a birder's paradise.

FAIRBANKS, Alaska (left)

A ceremonial game played on a blanket of skins, the blanket toss has an important role in the *Nalukatak*, the festival that draws the spring whaling season to a close. Traditionally held by *umialiks* (boat-owners) only if the preceding hunt was successful, the festival both honors the spirit of the whale and hopes for the success of future hunting seasons. The first person to be tossed into the air is the successful *umialik*.

SIERRA NEVADA, California (above)

The "Garden Wall," a natural barrier of mountain and desert that protects the extensive irrigation projects in central California, has its most formidable component in the Sierra Nevada, also known as the Range of Twilight. The subtle colors of twilight over Twin Lakes on the eastern slope of the range capture one moment in an ever-changing panorama of mountain light.

SKAGIT RIVER, Washington

The Skagit River delta, south of Mount
Vernon in western Washington, boasts
some of the state's most productive land.
The agricultural flats are reclaimed
swampland maintained by a complex
system of dikes, pumps and tide gates.
The tractor gives a sense of the size of
these tulip fields in April bloom.

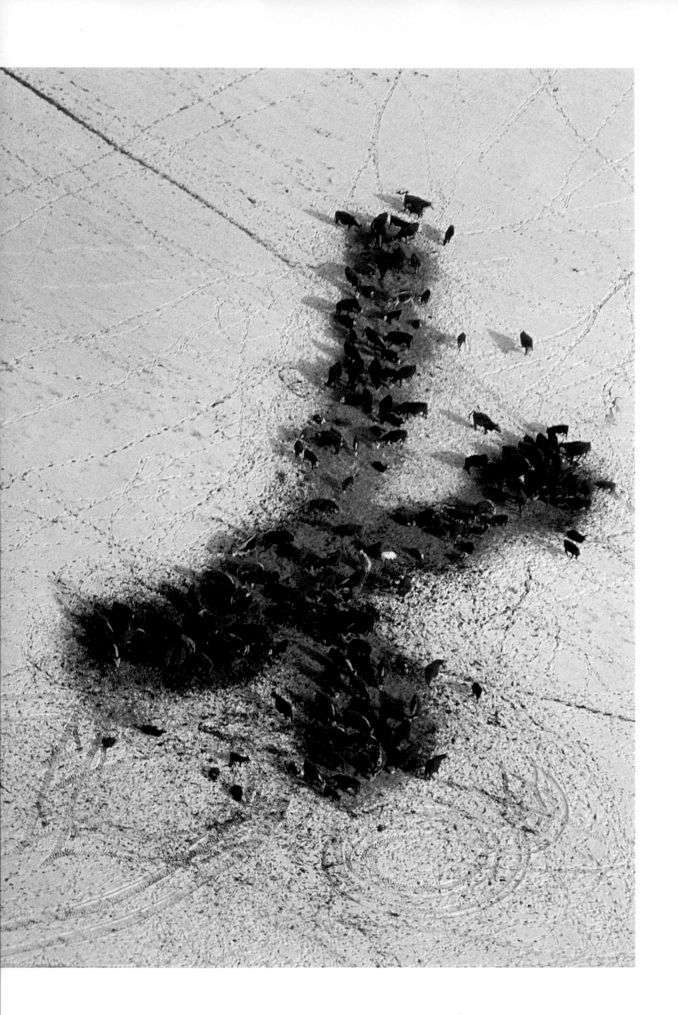

MODOC COUNTY, California (left)

Hay and hungry cattle form an X against the Surprise Valley snow. In the harsh climate of the Modoc Plateau, summer heat can exceed 100 degrees, while winter brings snow and sub-zero temperatures. Averaging more than 4,000 feet in elevation, the geologically spectacular Modoc Plateau extends from northeastern California west toward the Cascade Range.

SEATTLE, Washington (right)

Seattle's central position on Puget Sound helped it to win control of shipping and eventual dominance of the regional economy. The days of small boats—the mosquito fleet—are recalled during Maritime Week in May. The annual tugboat race on Elliott Bay is a major attraction.

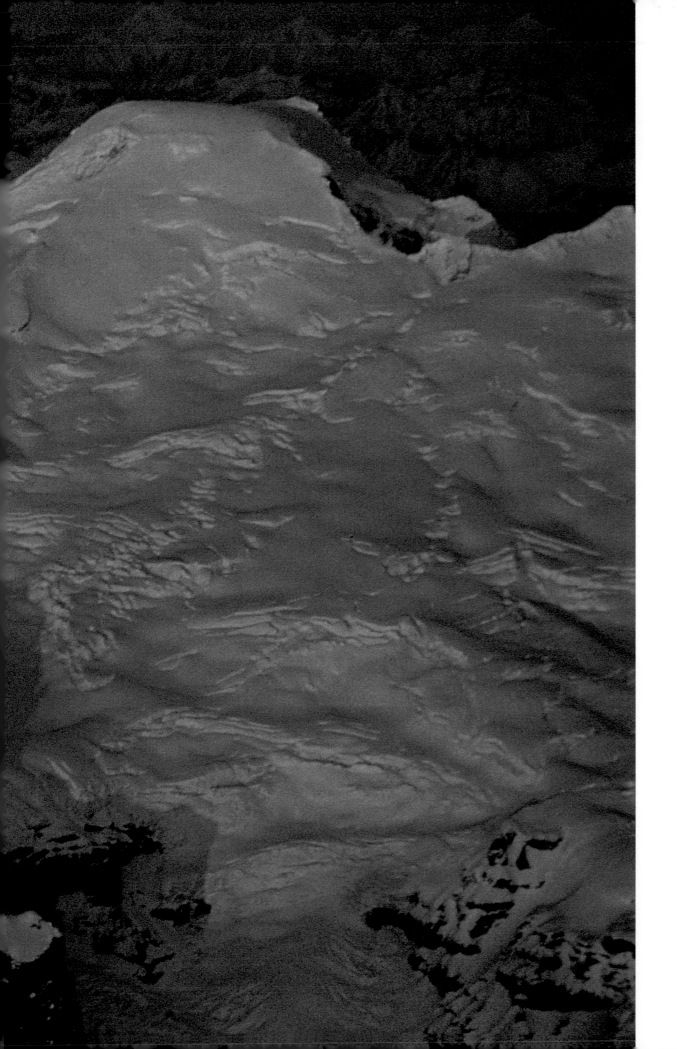

MOUNT BAKER, Washington

The Indians called Mount Baker *Komo Kulshan*, "the steep white mountain," because of the heavy glaciation around the cone. Here the northwest flank of Washington's northernmost volcano, seen from the southwest in winter, and with a full moon rising, is bathed in alpenglow.

TACOMA, Washington (left)

For years Tacoma called itself the "lumber capital of the world," its sawmills cutting lumber for places as diverse as China, Australia and Japan. But the old sawmills disappeared with the first-growth timber. Logs by the tens of thousands still find their way to Commencement Bay, but those that are not chipped into pulp are shipped whole to Japan, where they are milled to dimensions not cut by American sawmills.

DAYTON, Oregon (right)

Sprinklers spray water over approximately 1,000 acres of orderly plant rows at the Monrovia Nursery, near Dayton in the Willamette Valley. The nursery, one of the town's largest employers, produces more than 2,000 varieties of perennials, shrubs, trees, vines, ferns and grasses to supply the Pacific Northwest.

HAWAIIAN ISLANDS

HAWAII ∾ KAUAI ∾ MAUI ∾ MOLOKAI ∾ NIIHAU ∾ OAHU

The last state admitted into the union, this volcanic archipelago approximately 2,400 miles west of the continental United States still retains the feel of a familiar yet exotic outpost. American fast food chains, fashions and popular culture vie with Polynesian snack stalls, bright aloha shirts and mellow hula music. Hawaii's cultural fusion is a legacy of its historic role as a trade stop between North America and Australasia.

Although the Hawaiian archipelago comprises 137 islands, its eight easternmost islands—Hawaii, Oahu, Molokai, Kauai, Maui and Niihau, as well as the virtually uninhabited Lanai and the totally uninhabited Kahoolawe—account for more than 99 percent of the state's land area and are typically considered to be Hawaii proper. Topographically spectacular, the islands are the tops of massive submerged volcanoes, built up by countless layers of lava. Streams have carved deep gorges through the mountains or eroded channels down the

sides of sea cliffs. Kauai boasts two of the state's most noted examples: the Waimea Canyon and the lush, cliff-lined Na Pali coast.

The island group was originally settled by Polynesians who crossed vast expanses of water in open canoes. The first European to set foot in Hawaii was the English explorer James Cook in 1778. News of the lush tropical islands spread, and they soon became an important way-station for whalers and other Pacific Rim traders. Protestant missionaries followed in their wake and set about converting the natives to Christianity.

Planters were more interested in the islands' rich volcanic soil and warm climate. The first sugar plantation was established in 1837; by the end of the century, Hawaii was a major sugar and pineapple exporter. The plantation owners grew increasingly influential and demanding, and eventually forced the island's monarchy to accept an elected

PELEKUNU VALLEY, Molokai

Some geologists theorize that the high cliffs of Pelekunu Valley were carved by a massive earthquake, which cracked the old volcano and dumped the northern half of the shield into the sea. They cite as evidence submerged debris slides reaching into the Hawaiian deep. The prevailing theory, however, is that pounding surf undercut the cliffs, causing the upper rock to shear off and collapse.

government controlled by the business sector. The monarchy was overthrown entirely in 1893. Hawaii became a United States territory five years later, and finally was admitted into the union as a state in 1959.

The planters' influence also extended to other areas. To make up for a labor shortage on the islands, they brought in some 400,000 workers, primarily from Asia, in the period between 1852 and 1930. At the turn of the twentieth century, about three-quarters of the islands' population was of Asian origin. Since the 1930s, however, the state's new arrivals have come primarily from the American mainland, and Caucasians (or part-Caucasians) now constitute almost half the population.

While they share common geological foundations, the islands each have their own character. Oahu is by far the most developed. Maui and the Big Island of Hawaii have small towns and remote wilderness preserves in the shadow of active volcanoes. Molokai lies off the beaten track and is more tranquil. Niihau is privately owned by one company.

KOHALA, Hawaii (left)

A sinuous black band of asphalt and manicured landscaping slashes through sunset-reddened lava. The offset white pyramids at top signal the entrance from Queen Kaahumanu Highway to Anaehoomalu Bay and the Hilton Waikoloa Village resort. Kohala is the oldest of the volcanoes on the Big Island.

WAIKOLOA, Hawaii (above)

A collection of geometric shapes arranged along the Big Island's rugged Kohala coast: the Hilton Waikoloa Village. About the pool, one tourist said, "It's so close to the ocean you could throw a seashell into it." Most of Hawaii's visitors remain poolside because they prefer the safety and comfort of easy access and the proximity of the bar.

HANAUMA BAY, Oahu (above)

Once a remote, pristine spot frequented only by fishermen, Hanauma Bay has become too popular. Every year up to 3 million visitors come, most shuttled in by tour companies operating out of Waikiki, 10 miles away. In 1967 the bay became an underwater park, and fishing was banned. By 1990 so many people had come to see and feed the tame fish and had so fouled the place with trash and stirred-up silt that access restrictions had to be implemented.

HONOLULU, Oahu (right)

Reaching ever higher to catch a glimpse of the ocean, the high rises of Waikiki Beach dominate Honolulu's skyline. These blue waters contrast sharply with the stagnant Ala Wai Canal, at front. Developers, in a campaign against the perceived threat of mosquitoes caused by the marshes, streams, taro ponds and rice fields, began diverting water into the 2-mile-long Ala Wai Canal. A government-sponsored cleanup is currently underway to regenerate the watershed.

KAMAOA WIND FARM, Hawaii (left)

Mitsubishi wind generators power the Kamaoa Wind Farm, South Point, on Hawaii's Big Island. As a power source, Hawaii's prevailing trade winds (which blow almost year-round) excite every environmentalist. Built in 1986 on a former cattle property, this wind farm provides approximately 14 million kilowatt hours of electricity to Hawaii Electric Light Company, which is enough to power about 7,000 homes.

HONOLULU, Oahu (right)

Variously described as a cement beehive or a stack of coasters, the Contessa condominium rises high above Moiliili, a suburb near the University of Hawaii. Its proximity to the university makes the Contessa a popular rental choice for local and international students.

KUPAIANAHA, Hawaii

"The blood of the earth" scabs over in a lava sink at Kilauea. Such depressions occur when a subterranean tube of fast-moving *pahoehoe* (liquid) lava burns a cooled flow above. Residents can tell how active eruptive phases are by the way helicopter traffic increases. "It starts to look like a war zone, there are so many choppers coming in," says a geologist at Hawaii Volcanoes Observatory.

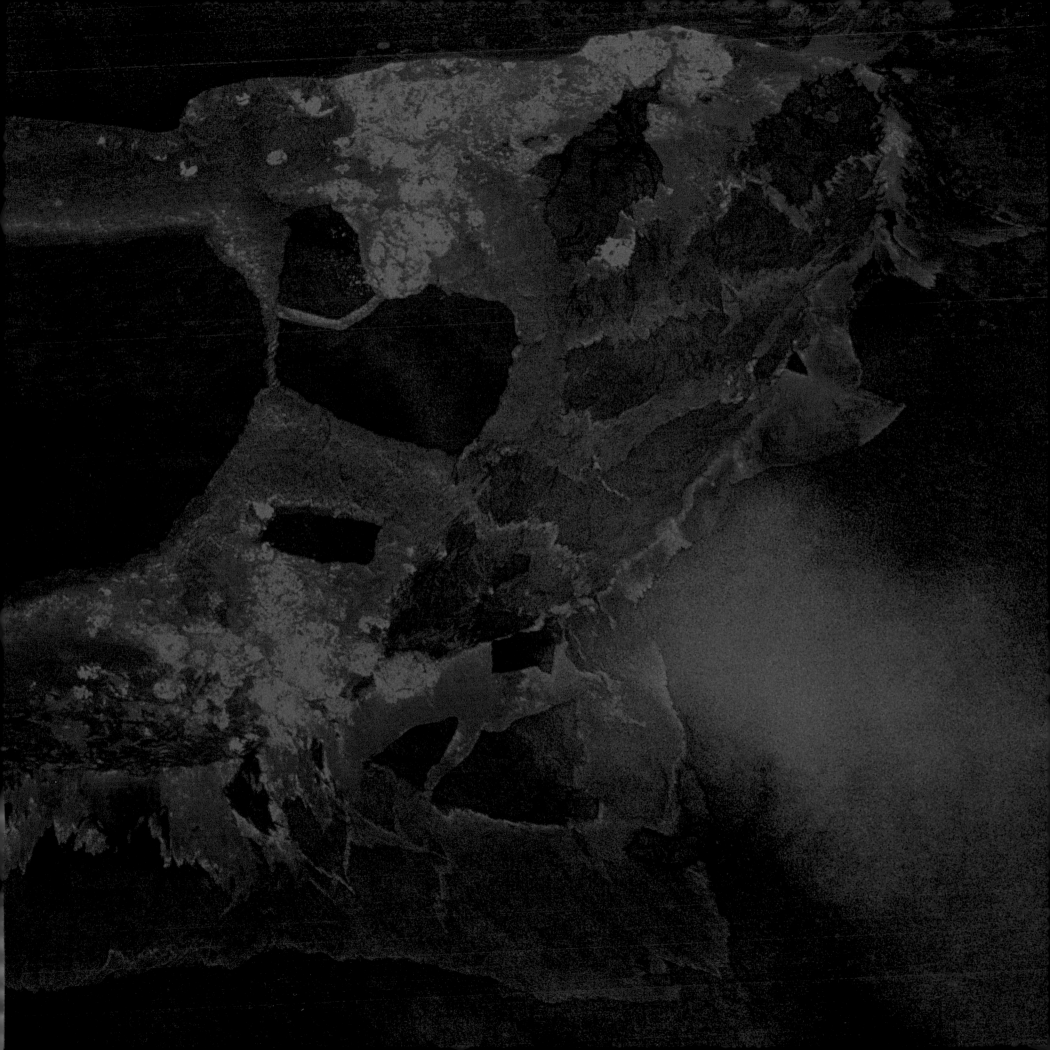

WAIKIKI, Oahu (left)

The surf report for Waikiki this day was "flat to a foot." Surfing has been central to Hawaiian culture for centuries, with all sections of society—men and women, commoners and royalty—participating in the sport. Petroglyphs carved into rock faces on many of the Hawaiian islands, along with ancient chants and oral history, tell of the Hawaiian passion for surfing.

WAIMEA CANYON, Kauai (right)

Pinnacles and bluffs, like these in Waimea Canyon are the remains of volcanic cones of dense, erosion-resistant lava. Known as the "Grand Canyon of the Pacific," Waimea Canyon was formed by the conflicting processes of erosion, sporadic volcanic activity and seismic shifts. A trough bent from ancient fault lines paved the way for wind and rain to gouge weather-beaten shapes into the hill slopes, which over time were partially filled by more lava.

HAWAIIAN ISLANDS

HALEAKALA, Maui (left)

The Haleakala Observatory, colloquially known as Science City, is located on the summit of Haleakala volcano. Lasers fired from these domes and other objects in near space have measured distances and provided scientists with information useful in developing missile defense systems. Though the last eruption here occurred in 1790, the Haleakala volcano is dramatic evidence of the Hawaiian islands' fiery origins.

PUUHONUA O HONAUNAU NATIONAL HISTORICAL PARK, Hawaii (above)

Originally constructed in 1650, the Hale o Keawe temple is a monument to ancestral chiefs at *Puuhonua* (place of refuge). Bounded by a wall 10 feet high and almost 1,000 feet long, this complex of royal palaces and temple structures was a place of spiritual absolution for those who broke tribal law, and a refuge for Hawaiians until the nineteenth century.

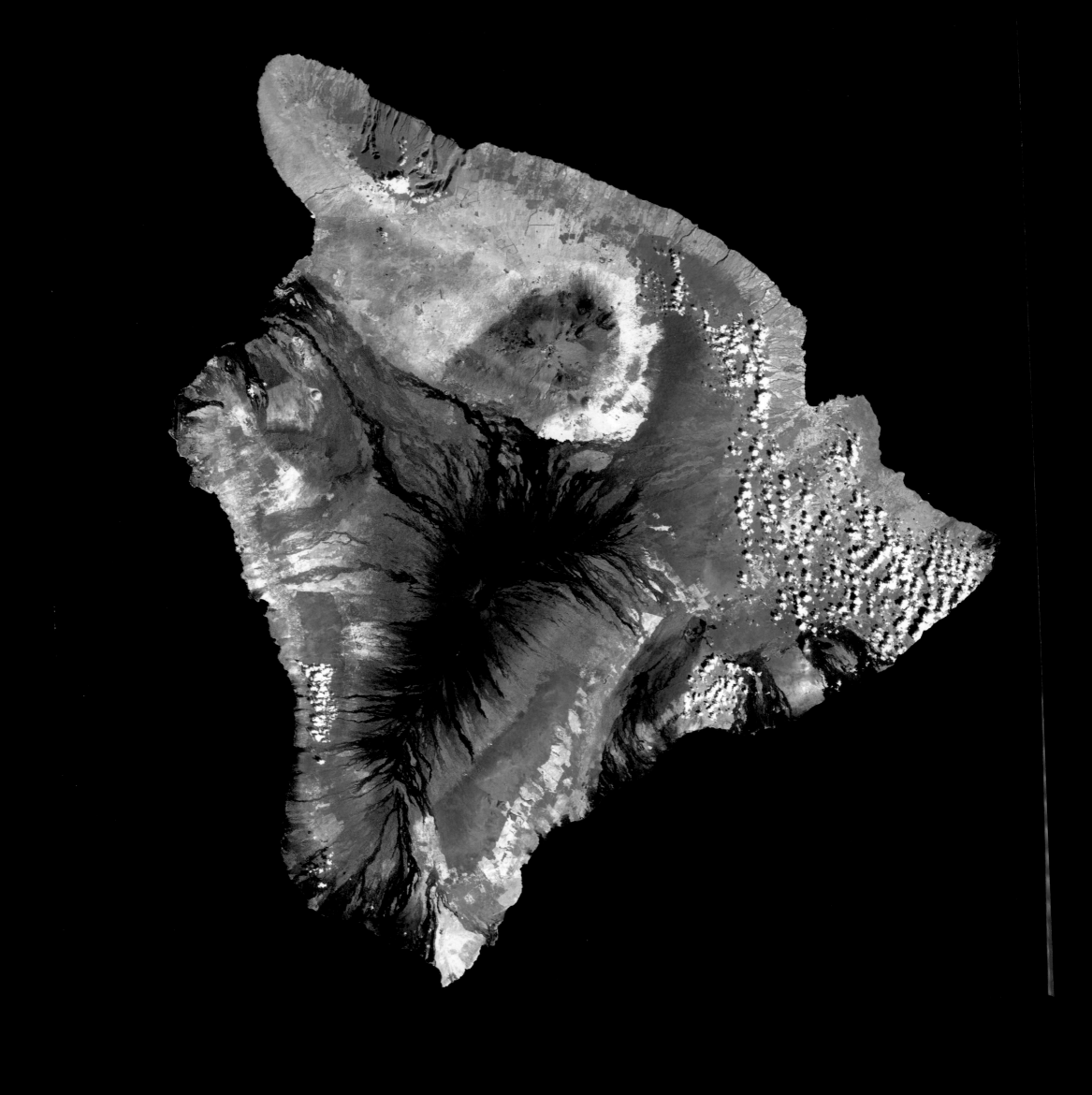

BIG ISLAND, Hawaii (left)

Seen here isolated from the surrounding
ocean, this Landsat satellite image of
Hawaii's Big Island was compiled from data
collected from 1999 to 2001. The island is
dominated by the ancient black lava of the
central Mauna Loa volcano, while smoke
from the steady eruptions of Mauna Kilauea
appears blue. Supported by the rich volcanic
soil, tropical forests are shades of green.

AKAKA FALLS, Hawaii (right)

A layer of dense basalt resists the erosive
force of Akaka Falls in the South Hilo
district of the Big Island. The plunge-pool
action at the waterfall's base has eaten a
deep cavity into the softer rock below.
Aerial access to the mountainous centers
of the main islands can be limited by dense
cloud and variable wind conditions.

HONOLULU, Oahu

At the Kahala Mandarin Oriental Hotel, on
Oahu's south shore, a dredged reef and
artificial peninsula and island give tourists
a safe venue for ocean activities. The hotel
also boasts a natural lagoon that is home
to bottlenose dolphins, green sea turtles
and tropical fish, enabling tourists to catch
a glimpse of Hawaii's wildlife without
having to leave the hotel.

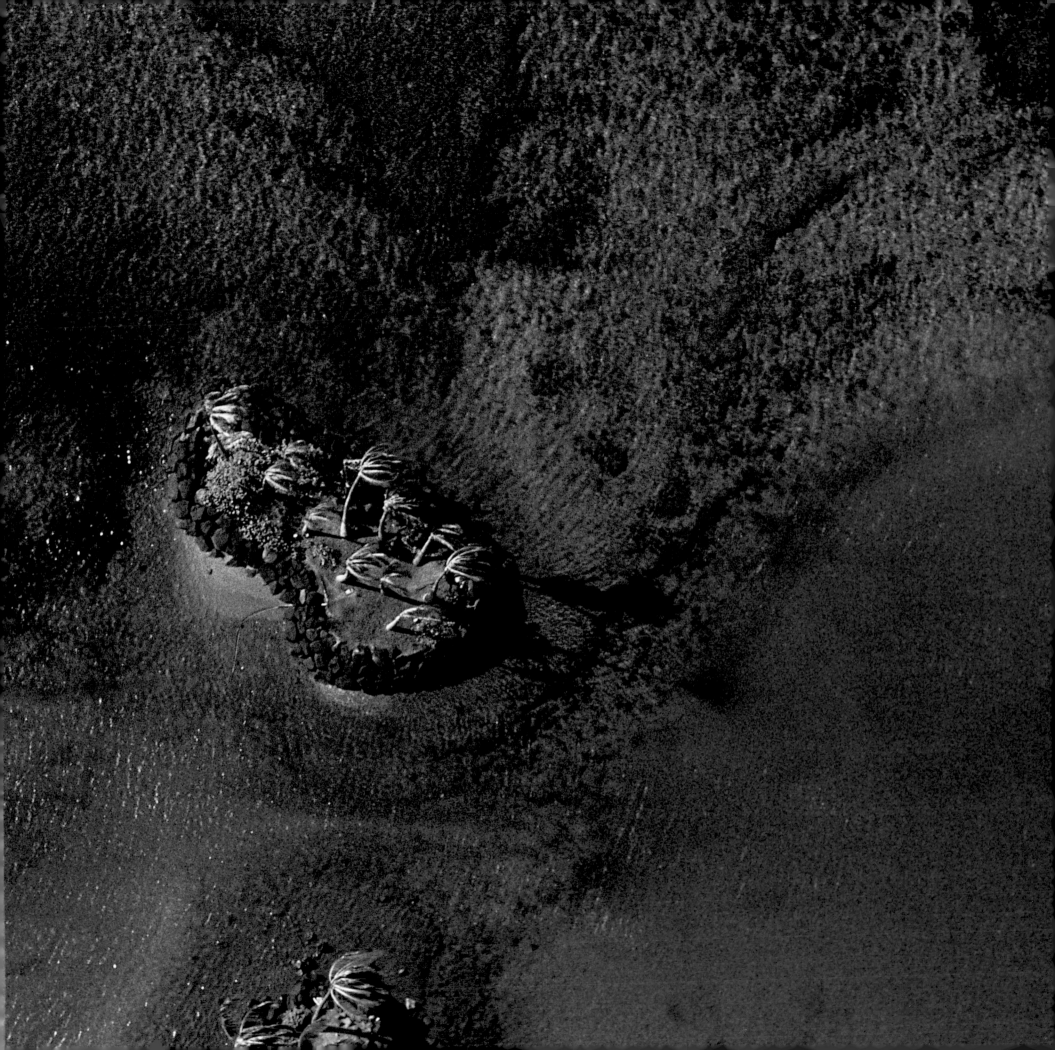

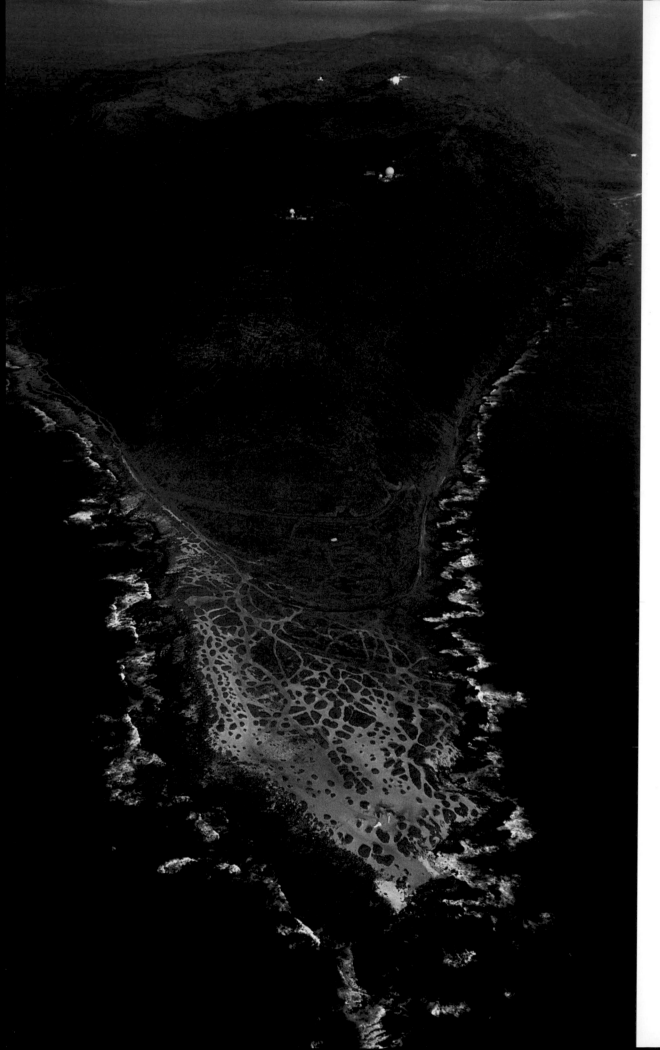

KAENA POINT, Oahu (left)

Like a barbed tip of a warrior's spear, Kaena Point aims toward the heart of Kauai, a hundred miles away. For ancient Hawaiians, Kaena was a *leina-a-ka-uhane*, a land's end where the souls of the dead leaped into the spirit world. The point and its lowland dunes have been protected as a Natural Area Reserve since 1983.

MAKUA VALLEY, Oahu (right)

One of the last undeveloped valleys on Oahu, Makua is a typical amphitheater-headed valley exhibiting alluvium slopes and fluted walls. Since 2001, the United States Army and environmentalists have been working together to protect this former military training site from serious ecological damage.

HAWAIIAN ISLANDS

INDEX

Weldon Owen wishes to thank the following people for their help with this project: Jennifer Losco, Puddingburn Editorial Services (index)
Photography Wm. Ervin, Leo Meier, Reg Morrison, Steven Proehl
All photography is copyright Weldon Owen Inc. except: 47, 76–7, 82, 86, 98, 103, 119, 130, 139, 142, 150, 153 APL/CBT; 6, 7, 9, 12, 24, 25, 34, 35, 40–1, 50, 54, 69, 70–1, 71, 72–3, 74, 75, 78, 79, 80–1, 83, 84–5, 87, 88–9, 90, 93, 94, 95, 96, 97, 99, 123, 127, 131, 135, 136–7, 143, 147, 151, 152, 157, 168, 184, 189 Cameron Davidson; 155, 160, 172, 181 Bill Ellzey; 92, 101, 104–5, 112–3, 115, 120–1, 129, 132–3, 134, 138, 140–1, 144–5, 148–9, 166–7, 177, 178–9, 180, 186–7, 192, 196, 202–3, 206–7, 216, 218–9, 224, 229, 233 Getty Images; 169, 188, 190–191 Charles O'Rear; 2–3, 6, 26, 102, 108–9, 111, 114, 116–7, 118, 121, 122, 124–5, 126 Jerry Stebbins; 007, 010–1, 195, 198–9, 201, 205, 209, 210–1, 213, 214–5, 221, 226–7, 230–1, 232 Harald Sund; 20, 62, 91, 107, 110, 146, 173, 217, 248 TPL/SPL
Maps Encompass Graphics